Monographic Journals of the Near East *Afroasiatic Linguistics* 8/3 (November 1982)

THE DEVELOPMENT OF THE PARTICIPLE IN BIBLICAL, MISHNAIC, AND MODERN HEBREW

by

Amnon Gordon
Los Angeles, California

The Hebrew participle undergoes polarization; from an "intermediate" form with some nominal and some verbal qualities in Biblical Hebrew, it develops to become, in modern Hebrew, either clearly nominal or clearly verbal in any given case. The paper traces this process. This development is closely related to other issues. For example, when the dual time reference system of Biblical Hebrew becomes the tripartite tense system evident in Modern Hebrew, the participle, having a basic time reference to general time to begin with, fills the vacuum created in the verb system by becoming the present tense. Since the participle always involves SVO order, its entrance into the verb system contributes significantly to the shift in Hebrew from VSO to SVO order. The change in the participle also gives rise to the only construction in Hebrew which utilizes an auxiliary verb.

Table of Contents

1. INTRODUCTION

This paper traces the development of the Hebrew participle through Biblical Hebrew (BH), Mishnaic Hebrew (MH), and Modern Hebrew (MnH), the three major periods in the history of Hebrew in which Hebrew was and is used as a living, everyday language.

I shall show that the participle first appears as a form which is, so to speak, a semi-verb, i.e. lacking an important quality that verbs have–inherent reference to time (for an explanation of this term, see section 2.2.1. below). As such it can easily be used as a noun or an adjective. From that stage the participle develops to become a regular verb. Simultaneously, some of its manifestations develop to become lexicalized nouns, with no more verbal overtones than other, non-participial nouns might have. Tracing this development will provide the opportunity to discuss some other interesting processes in the development of the Hebrew verb system.

The observation that the BH participle was of a different nature than its MH and MnH counterparts is not a new one. I shall mention below various references to the literature where conclusions that I reach are paralleled by observations of various writers. My purpose in this paper is to study the subject in much greater detail. I should, however, mention the work of Givón (1977), which examines BH. Givón says that the participle shifts from being a nominal form to being a verbal form, but this is not the main focus of his study. His main interest in the participle is from the point of view of the shift which he asserts has occurred in BH from an aspect system to a tense system.

The periods represented by the texts that I analyze are, very generally,

Early BH (EBH)–11th to 6th Century BC.
Late BH (LBH)–6th to 5th Century BC.
MH–4th Century BC to 2nd Century AD (but the text was edited and given final form only towards the end of the period)

For MnH I used no text but rather my native speaker competence and information from a few consultants. The period reflected is roughly the last thirty years, with the greatest emphasis on the very recent usages.

Although much time separates the MH period and the beginning of MnH (late 19th Century), continuity in the language was preserved by the fact that in the revival of Hebrew in modern Israel, Biblical and Mishnaic Hebrew were used as the starting point. More about this point in the chapter on MnH (Chapter 4).

2. BIBLICAL HEBREW

2.1. Synopsis of the investigation

2.1.1. Background

The texts surveyed for this chapter are

Genesis (abbr. Gn.), first 10 chapters
I Samuel (abbr. I S), first 10 chapters
I Kings (abbr. I R), first 10 chapters
Song of Solomon (abbr. Cant.), the whole text
Ecclesiastes (abbr. Eccl.), first 10 chapters
Nehemiah (abbr. Neh.), first 10 chapters

The first three represent Early Biblical Hebrew, the last three represent Late Biblical Hebrew.

In order to describe the participle it is necessary to explain that EBH utilizes a dual system, which has been regarded in the literature as either a tense or an aspect system. The verb can assume a perfect or past function (depending on whether one accepts the "aspect" view or the "tense" view), or it can assume an imperfect/non-past function. I shall use the terms "perfect" and "imperfect" without claiming thereby that EBH verbs do not convey tense. Morphologically, the verb has a suffixed form and a prefixed form, used for the perfect and for the imperfect, respectively. There is also a "converted" form, in which a "*waw* conversive" is added to the suffixed and the prefixed forms reversing their function to imperfect and perfect, respectively. The perfect and imperfect constitute the finite system. The participle is a non-finite form, the exact nature of which I will examine below.

In MnH, and to a large extent in MH, that dual system has been replaced by a tripartite system of tense. The suffixed form clearly serves as the MnH past tense; the prefixed form serves as the future tense; and the participle has become the present tense, thus joining the finite system.

In Hebrew the participle is called *benoni*, or the "intermediate" form, and indeed in EBH it is a form between a verb and a nominal (by nominal I mean a noun or an adjective, which are similar in Hebrew). Morphologically, the participle is noun-like. Like a noun, it has four declined forms, reflecting gender and number, while verbs have eight or nine forms, reflecting gender, number, and person. These morphological facts remained constant throughout the history of Hebrew; as we shall see, the change in the participle does not affect its morphology. Below is an example utilizing the root *gnb*, which means, as a verb, 'steal', and as a noun, 'a thief'.

VERB IN PERFECT (Verb in imperfect has parallel paradigm)

Singular		Plural	
I	*ganavti*	we	*ganavnu*
you m.	*ganavta*	you m.	*ganavtem*
you f.	*ganavt*	you f.	*ganavten*
he	*ganav*	they	*ganvu*
she	*ganva*		

PARTICIPLE		NOUN		
masc. sing.	*gonev*	masc. sing.	*ganav*	'thief'
fem. sing.	*gonevet*	fem. sing.	*ganevet*	'thief'
masc. pl.	*gonvim*	masc. pl.	*ganavim*	'thieves'
fem. pl.	*gonvot*	fem. pl.	*ganavot*	'thieves'

This example is rendered in MnH pronunciation, but it is typical of all historical stages of the language. The sounds [b] and [v] are here allophones of the same phoneme. No gloss is provided for the participles because, of course, this is the subject of the whole paper. Generally, however, the meaning of a participle is somewhere between 'he/she/they are doing the action designated by the verb' and 'he/she/they who do that action'.

Further similarity of the participle to a noun is its ability to appear in a construct, a possessive construction, in the role of the "possessed", e.g.

yošev *ohalim*[1]
dwellPAR of tents
'one who dwells in tents'

The form of this possessive construction (here rendered in its MnH pronunciation) has never changed since EBH and until MnH.

So far I have shown two examples of how the participle is noun-like: its morphology and its ability to appear in a possessive construction. More examples and analysis will follow. I add now that the participle can also appear in slots otherwise reserved for adjectives. The following two examples are from BH, but are again typical of all stages of the language.

Adjective as postnominal modifier:

gɛšɛm *kåḇeḏ* (I R. 18.45)
rain heavy
'heavy rain'

Participle as postnominal modifier:

gɛšɛm *šo^{w}ṭep̄* (Ezechiel 13.11)
rain sweepPAR
'sweeping rain, driving rain'

Finally, the participle can also function as a verb–except that, in BH, it lacks one feature that verbs have, namely, reference to time (whether through aspect or through tense). Details will follow below.

2.1.2. The Direction of the Investigation and the Nature of the Text

In BH it is already possible to see evidence of reanalysis of the participle. From the state of a semi-verb that may be interpreted in many cases as being both verbal and nominal, it is slowly being reanalyzed as a regular, time-referenced verb, or, if it is not a full-fledged verb, then it is simply a nominal (a noun or an adjective). Further, the reanalyzed participle in its verbal capacity is a productive form. In MnH, for a newly coined verb, the participle is the automatic present tense. However, in its reanalyzed nominal capacity in MnH, it is unpredictable. It may be, say, the agent noun for the new verb, but then again other nominal patterns rather than the participle may well fulfill this function. Since early signs of the reanalysis in this direction are present throughout BH, one must conclude that the reanalysis began before the earliest stage reflected in the Bible. The reasons for the reanalysis will emerge in the course of the discussion below.

For the analysis of the participle I established a few parameters of investigation, and applied them to the texts and to MnH. The results of the investigation are given in the form of frequency and percentage tables with an accompanying discussion for BH and MH and a discussion for MnH. Each parameter is discussed in a different section.

I must address the question of the various books being far from ideal data. To begin with, they represent different genres: narrative, philosophical reflection, and poetry. However, the question that I am investigating seems to be rather unaffected by most of the peculiarities of genre. It is hard to imagine a writer so eccentric that he would utilize, say, a tripartite tense system when everyone else uses a dual system, or that he would change the time-reference clues,

---

[1] I shall gloss the participles with the suffix PAR so as to avoid the choice between glossing them as nouns or as verbs, either of which options would add unwanted coloring to the meaning of the word.

described below, arbitrarily and on his own. It is equally as hard to imagine the editors of the scriptures allowing such idiosyncrasy in the texts. The nature of the participle is not essentially a stylistic question.

However, and this is a more consequential point: it is possible that different dialects are represented in the different LBH books. This view has been advanced in the literature. In the southern part of ancient Israel, where Jerusalem, the capital, was located, a somewhat learned dialect of Hebrew developed and was used as the official dialect of the kingdom. Yet in the north the local dialect, closer to Aramaic and Phoenician, prevailed (see Rabin (1960:13-14; 1972: 21-22)).

One must keep in mind that in the LBH period the kingdom had split into two (930 B.C.); each of the two kingdoms underwent devastating wars and eventually fell (the last war, with the Romans, ending in 70 B.C.). While EBH flourished in a unified kingdom and is thus a uniform dialect, LBH reflects a decentralized language. Dialects that one would not have used in writing in the time of the unified kingdom were now used freely by some writers, whereas others still tried to imitate the venerable EBH style. There is also the possibility that Aramaic exercised considerable influence on LBH (see Bendavid (1967:60, 125-129)).

Thus it is possible that Nehemiah, Ecclesiastes, and Song of Solomon are written in dialects that are different from one another and from EBH (see Segal (1909:52-53) and Bendavid (1967: 77-79) regarding Nehemiah; Rabin (1960:27) and Bendavid (1967:77-79) regarding Ecclesiastes; Peretz (1967:26) regarding Song of Solomon).

As a result, it is difficult to compare the various LBH books and establish order among them with accuracy. This difficulty is freely admitted in the literature (see, for example, all of Margolis (1948), especially p. 77; Rabin (1960:7-8); and the Encyclopedia Judaica (1972, vol. 4:832-836).

Therefore, I shall not base my conclusions on order among these books, but only on the fact that they all follow EBH and precede MH.

2.2. Time Reference

2.2.1. Clues for Recognizing Time Reference; Terms Explained

This section deals with the reference of the participle to time. I shall use the terms "preceding", "concurrent", and "subsequent" to indicate time reference. My terms are to be understood as "preceding, concurrent, and subsequent to the time of speech, or the time of narration". These distinctions are clear throughout BH.

I shall refer to a verb as "having tense", or as "tensed", or as having an inherent time reference, when its very morphology is enough to establish its time reference. By contrast, the EBH participle has no tense; in its verbal use, its time reference comes in other ways.

Most of the clues that point to a time reference for a participle are context-dependent. Genesius (1855: §134), Bergsträsser (1926:425), and Driver (1892:166) recognize the importance of the context in determining time reference for the participle, but the dispense with the topic in a few sentences.

Following is a discussion of the clues for recognizing time reference in BH.

2.2.1.1. Time Indicator

Some participles receive their time reference from a special indicator in the context. It may be an adverb:

wayhi^{y}	*bayyo*^{w}*m*	*hahu'*	*wə'eli*	*šoꝁeƀ*	*bimqo*^{w}*mo*^{w}
and was	in the day	the that	and Eli	liePAR	in his place

'on that day as Eli lay in his bed'

'LiePAR' refers to the same time to which 'on that day' refers, i.e. preceding time.

Another time indicator which establishes concurrent time is the demonstrative *wəhinneʰ* 'and behold' (Bergsträsser (1926:425), too, mentions this word as helping to establish time reference, but with little discussion). In the Book of Kings Nathan the prophet tells King Solomon how Adonijah called his rebels together:

wəhinnåm	*'okliʸm*	*wəšotiʸm*	*ləpånåw*
and behold them	eatPAR	and drinkPAR	before him

'and they are eating and drinking before him'

Time here is established as concurrent. Were the demonstrative and subject replaced by a subject alone–say, *wəhem* 'and they'–the participle could be interpreted as preceding; it would take on the time of the narrative, which is the time-referencing clue discussed next.

2.2.1.2. The Narrative

When an indicator is present, the reference to time is explicit. When no indicator is present, the participle will be understood to refer to the time of the narrative–whether expressed by a higher verb in the same sentence or in other sentences. That, then, is an implicit reference to time.

waya'ălu	*kɔl*	*hå'åm*	*'ahăråw*	*wəhå'åm*	*məhalləliʸm*	*bahăliliʸm*
and went up	all	the people	after him	and the people	playPAR	in flutes

'and all the people came after him, playing flutes'

The participle refers to preceding time, as expressed by the verb 'went up'.

Clearly, then, time is assigned by a complex mechanism, combining morphology, syntax, and pragmatics, too, as seen in the next time-assigning clue.

2.2.1.3. Inference

At times no indicator is present, nor can the narrative time be applied to the participle. Rather, the time reference can be inferred from the context. In these cases, replacing the participle with a tensed verb which indicates a time reference other than the inferred one would change the meaning.

šə'elåʰ	*'aḥat*	*qətannåʰ*	*'ånokiʸ*	*šo'elet*	*me'ittåk*	(I R.2.20)
a request	one	small	I	request	from with you	

'I am making one small request of you'.

Obviously, preceding or subsequent time will not correctly replace the concurrent reference inferred here.

Another example: Nehemiah begins to ask a favor of the king of Babylon without actually getting to the point. The king urges Nehemiah to get to the point:

'al	*maʰ*	*zzeʰ*	*'attåʰ*	*məbaqqeš*	(Neh. 2.4)
on	what	this	you	requestPAR?	

'what is it that you are asking for?'

Nehemiah then completes his request to rebuild Jerusalem. 'RequestPAR' can therefore refer only to concurrent time. Substituting, say, the perfect or past form of the verb (rendering 'What is it that you asked for?') would change the meaning; it would mean that the king believed Nehemiah to have completed his request but that the request was not clear to the king.

Note that the process of inference, while similar to the "time of the narrative" clue discussed above in relying on the context, is also different from it. The narrative clue is a mechanical transfer of the time reference of, say, a higher verb to the participle, while inference is a logical process which calls for a consideration of the meaning of the passage. Thus, in the last example above one must consider the fact that Nehemiah was in the middle of his request when the king asked his question.

2.2.1.4. Unbounded

This is perhaps the most interesting situation. As in the case of inference, no indicator is present nor is the narrative time applicable; however, the participle cannot be regarded as having a narrowly bounded inferred time reference such as preceding, concurrent, or subsequent, because assigning any one of these, arbitrarily, to the participle, or replacing the participle with any tensed form of the verb, will not clash with its meaning as we perceive it in the text. Such arbitrary reference assignment will not create a paraphrase of the original phrase, but it will create a meaning not contradictory to the original one. For example:

ʼăđonåy *memi^{y}t* *umәhayye^{h}* (I S.2.6)
God cause to diePAR and cause to come to lifePAR
'God causes to die and brings to life'

This is from a song glorifying God; obviously God is not causing to die or bringing to life at the moment of singing only. It is also not contradictory to the sentence to say that God has caused to die and brought to life before and will again do so after the moment of speech.

It seems to me that in such cases there is indeed no clue that assigns time reference to the participle, and in the absence of such a clue the participle appears in its true character–its unmarked form with regard to time reference. It appears as potentially having all possible time references, or GENERAL TIME. I will refer to such time reference as unbounded, since it appears only in the absence of any clue that narrows down the time reference to a more limited scope.

I find that here I am in accord with Driver (1892:167) who states, "When there is nothing to imply that the state denoted by the participle extends beyond the moment of speaking, the force of the phrase is as nearly as possible that of the true English present." Notice that general time is different from concurrent. The former is not limited to a specific time reference; the latter holds only at the moment of speech. Of all participles, the general participle is closest, of course, to nouns and adjectives, as they too have no time reference. I should perhaps say that I do not regard nouns and adjectives as having general time, only as close to general time participles in not being limited to a specific time reference. Once again, pragmatics as well as syntax and morphology must play a part in establishing a participle as unbounded. Following is another example:

diƀrey *hăꝁåmi^{y}m* *bәnahaŧ* *nišmåʻi^{y}m* (Eccl. 9.17)
words of wise PL in quiet are heardPAR
'the words of wise people are heard restfully'

Here a general truth is expressed, and again, no time is provided by the context nor is it contradictory to the sentence to replace the participle with preceding- or subsequent-time verbs (although, again, such replacement will not create a paraphrase). Again we have general time, arrived at because the participle is unbounded.

While all unbounded participles are general, NOT ALL GENERAL PARTICIPLES ARE UNBOUNDED. Other clues that impart the general time are the narrative, adverbials, and semantic context.

The whole narrative may be in the general time, which the participle adopts too:

ʼeyn *kåmo^{w}ꝁå* *ʼĕlohi^{y}m* ... *šomer* *habbәri^{y}ŧ* (I R.8.23)
there is not like you God ... keepPAR of the covenant
'there is none like you, God ... (the one who) keeps the covenant'

"There is not" is a general time statement here, meaning 'there was not and will not be'. 'KeepPAR' reflects this time reference; it is general too (if the sentence began with 'there was not', in other words, if it had preceding time, the participle would reflect that time reference and would have preceding time too).

Adverbs may also impart general time:

'ăḇåḏe^{y}ḵå	*'elle^{h}*	*hå'omḏi^{y}m*	*ləp̄åneḵå*	*tåmi^{y}ḏ*	(I R.10.8)
your slaves	these	that standPAR	before you	always	

'these slaves of yours that always stand before you'

'These', a demonstrative, would make the participle concurrent–perhaps the speaker was pointing at the slaves, who were standing there at the time of speech. However, 'always' indicates otherwise: 'standPAR' is general.

Semantic content of the participle is crucial in an example such as the following, from the description of God's creation of the Garden of Eden:

wayyaṣmaḥ	*'ăḏonåy*	*'ɛlohi^{y}m*	...	*kɔl*	*'eṣ*	...	*wənåhår*
and made grow	Lord	God	...	every	tree	...	and a river

yoṣe'	*me'eḏɛn*	(Gn.2.9-10)
goes outPAR	from Eden	

'and the Lord God made every tree grow ... and a river flowed out of Eden'

Obviously, the river did not flow out of Eden just once; the content of the sentence makes it clear that general time is implied. Notice, however, that since general time here is not created by unboundedness, IT IS ENTIRELY POSSIBLE FOR IT TO CO-OCCUR WITH ANOTHER TIME, here, the preceding time. 'Goes outPAR' is therefore both preceding and general.

2.2.1.5. Continuous

Here I marked those participles that would be translated with a continuous form in English, those cases where one action occurs while another action (the one rendered as continuous) is in progress. BH, of course, does not mark these with a special marker, and I doubt that the native speakers would recognize them as a separate category. The reason I established the continuous as a separate category in the table was so as to check if it operates in any unique way; but as the discussion below will show, it is possible to regard the continuous as a sub-category of the general without any significant changes in the conclusions drawn from the data. For example:

wayəhi^{y}	*šəmu^{w}'el*	*ma'ăle^{h}*	*hå'o^{w}lå^{h}*	*up̄lišti^{y}m*
and was	Shmuel	offerPAR	the burnt offering	and the Philistines

niggšu^{w}	*lammilḥåmå^{h}*	*bəyisrå'el*	(I S.7.10)
approached	to the war	in Israel	

'and as Samuel was offering the burnt offering, the Philistines approached to fight the Israelites'

Here the act of the sacrifice is a prolonged one; another act, the attack, suddenly happens while the first is in progress. This is a typical situation to be rendered with a continuous in English, as it is in the gloss above.

2.2.2. The Appearance of the Different Clues in the Texts and Conclusions

Below is Table 1. It presents, first, the numbers of participles in each book that get their time reference by each category, e.g. inference, indicator, etc. Second, it shows what time the participles refer to. The row entitled "How many of inference participles refer to concurrent time?" is interesting because eventually, when the participle becomes a verb, it will have no external time referencing clue, and it will refer mainly to concurrent time. The table shows that many inference participles ALREADY refer to concurrent time.

Of course, the same consideration is true of the unbounded participles. They too rely on no external clues. And indeed the question of what time the unbounded participles refer to is answered by the section of five rows devoted to the general participles, where we find that all unbounded participles are general ones, as I have already mentioned.

TABLE 1.
Time Reference

		BOOK	GN	I S	I R	CANT	ECCL	NEH	TOTAL
		TOTAL PARS IN CHAPTERS SURVEYED	22	59	61	19	55	75	291
HOW DOES THE PAR REFER TO TIME? (IN PARENTHESES: % OUT OF TOTAL TIME-REFERENCED PARS)		BY INFERENCE	2 (15.4)	5 (8.9)	4 (6.6)	3 (11.8)	1 (1.9)	29 (40.3)	44 (16.2)
		BY TIME INDICATOR	2 (15.4)	7 (12.5)	6 (10)	6 (35.3)	0 (0.0)	16 (22.2)	37 (13.6)
		BY NARRATIVE	5 (38.5)	33 (58.9)	46 (76.6)	6 (35.3)	0 (0.0)	22 (30.5)	112 (41.2)
		UNBOUNDED	4 (30.7)	11 (19.6)	4 (6.6)	2 (11.8)	53 (98.1)	5 (6.9)	79 (29.0)
		TOTAL TIME REFERENCED PARTICIPLES	13	56	60	17	54	72	272
WHAT TIME DOES THE PAR REFER TO? (IN PARENTHESES: PERCENTAGE AS ABOVE)		CONCURRENT	3 (23.0)	6 (10.7)	6 (10.0)	10 (58.8)	1 (1.9)	26 (36.1)	52 (19.1)
		HOW MANY REFERENCE PARS REFER TO CONCURRENT TIME?	2	3	3	3	1	26	38
		PRECEDING	5 (38.5)	28 (50.0)	43 (71.6)	2 (11.8)	0 (0.0)	37 (51.4)	115 (42.3)
		SUBSEQUENT	1 (7.7)	9 (16.0)	3 (5.0)	0 (0.0)	0 (0.0)	3 (4.2)	16 (5.9)
		GENERAL (MAY OVERLAP OTHER TIME REFERENCES)	8 (61.5)	19 (33.9)	20 (33.3)	5 (29.4)	53 (98.1)	32 (44.4)	137 (50.4)
		CONTINUOUS (ALWAYS OVERLAPS OTHER TIME REFERENCES)	0	13	1	1	0	1	16
	GENERAL	HOW MANY ARE EXCLUSIVE TIME REFERENCES (DO NOT OVERLAP)?	4 (30.8)	13 (23.2)	8 (13.3)	5 (29.4)	53 (98.1)	6 (8.3)	89 (32.7)
		OF THE ABOVE, HOW MANY UNBOUNDED?	4	11	4	2	53	5	79
		HOW MANY ARE GENERAL + PRECEDING?	4	6	12	0	0	16	38
		HOW MANY ARE GENERAL + CONCURRENT?	0	0	0	0	0	10	10
		HOW MANY ARE GENERAL + SUBSEQUENT?	0	0	0	0	0	0	0
	CONTINUOUS	HOW MANY ARE CONTINUOUS + PRECEDING?	0	13	1	1	0	1	16
		HOW MANY ARE CONTINUOUS + CONCURRENT?	0	0	0	0	0	0	0
		HOW MANY ARE CONTINUOUS + SUBSEQUENT?	0	0	0	0	0	0	0

I begin the discussion of the table by addressing myself to the first part, i.e. "How does the participle refer to time?" Consider the "By inference" row. There is a very noticeable rise in the number of inferred-time participles in Nehemiah: 40.3%. Out of the 29 constituting this percentage, 26 have concurrent time. Further, in Ecclesiastes and in Nehemiah, every single concurrent-time participle is an inferred-time one (see sixth and seventh rows).

Compare this state of affairs with Samuel and I Kings, where only half the concurrent-time participles are inferred-time ones. Clearly, in LBH the participle has reached a stage where it does not need an external clue (such as an adverb) or the narrative time reference to refer to concurrent time.

Notice now the amazing percentage of general participles in Ecclesiastes and the fact that all of them are unbounded. Of course, Ecclesiastes deals in generalities, but it does utilize the imperfect-future form quite often to express such generalities (see Givón (1977:223-224)). Another device, then, IS available for the purpose, a device which was used for that very purpose throughout BH; the rise in the percentage of participles used for that same purpose is therefore meaningful. The unbounded general time reference, once found in a small percentage of the participles (averaging 22.5% in EBH), has become the most natural time-reference to be associated with the participle in the consciousness of the speakers.

I should perhaps add that Ecclesiastes, despite the fact that it is a book of general, timeless wisdom, is by no means a book written exclusively in concurrent time. In the first three chapters, for example, one finds 82 verbs in the perfect, most of which actually refer to preceding time, as against 25 participles.

Simultaneously with the rise in unbounded habituals, the percentage of participles which rely on the narrative for their time reference decreases markedly, from 58% in EBH to 21.9% in LBH (note especially the 0% in Ecclesiastes).

There is a slight unexplained rise in the reliance on indicators: from 12.6% in EBH to 19.1% in LBH. Mostly, I think, this reluctance to dissociate the participle from an indicator as its time referencing device is due to the salient nature of the indicator. It is a tangible, easily perceived entity. The narrative, by contrast, is there not only–not even mainly–to give time reference; thus, it might more readily appear to the speakers that the time reference of the participle, which is in reality narrative-induced, is somehow self-understood. This is a situation where it is easier to start regarding the participle as having inherent time reference; easier, that is, than in those cases where a real word or affix (the indicator) is there mainly for the purpose of assigning time reference. Perhaps this is why the indicator is more reluctant to give way. Eventually, however, it does disappear, as in fact it does in Ecclesiastes and as we shall see it do in MH and in MnH. In all, then, the participle in LBH relies less and less on external markers and narrative time reference for its own time reference.

So far I discussed the means by which the participle refers to time. I move on now to the second part of the table, namely, "What time does the participle refer to?" I present here the percentages for EBH and LBH as two whole units rather than broken down as in the table.

Percentage of time-referenced participles that refer to

concurrent time:	EBH 11.6%
	LBH 25.9%
preceding time:	EBH 58.9%
	LBH 27.3%
subsequent time:	EBH 10%
	LBH 2%
general time:	EBH 36.4%
	LBH 62.9%

The obvious conclusion is that the participle refers less to preceding and subsequent time and more to concurrent and general time. Ecclesiastes is the most striking example of this trend, having no preceding or subsequent participles at all.

The next step in the development is for the time reference of the participle to stop being contextually determined (by unboundedness or by inference) and to start being inherent in the form itself or automatically associated with the form. At that stage we would say that the participle is a tensed verb.

We continue further down the table, to the five rows entitled "general", and find another interesting fact: the general time accompanies preceding time as an additional feature, i.e. a given participle refers to both preceding time and to general time in four of the books (it accompanies concurrent time only in Nehemiah, and it never accompanies subsequent time, probably because the narrative is usually in preceding time). However, in the Song of Solomon and in Ecclesiastes, general time occurs ONLY as the sole time reference of the participle. It appears, then, as a time reference in its own right, mutually exclusive of the others. This, of course, is the direction of development that I have claimed for the participle.

With respect to the rest of the table, I do not see significant trends. There is an unexplained large percentage of unbounded general participles in Genesis. There are also some appearances of continuous participles, all of which have the continuous feature accompanying some other time reference. As I explained above, I counted the continuous as a separate category mostly to examine if indeed it is one. I find that the data are too sporadic; apparently, the continuous is not a significant category in BH.

2.3. The Participle as a Nominal

2.3.1. The Data

Table 1 dealt with the verb-like characteristic of the participle, namely, its time reference. Table 2 below deals with the nominal quality of the participle, namely, its ability to fulfill the function of a noun or an adjective. The participle can appear as fulfilling both functions, nominal and verbal, in which case I refer to it as an "intermediate" form, as its Hebrew name (*benoni* 'one in the middle')[2] implies; or it may fulfill a nominal function with no verbal overtones.

TABLE 2.
Nominal Participles

<table>
<tr><td colspan="2">BOOK</td><td>GN</td><td>I S</td><td>I R</td><td>CANT</td><td>ECCL</td><td>NEH</td><td>TOTAL</td></tr>
<tr><td rowspan="2">THE PAR AS AN INTERMEDIATE FORM</td><td>ADJECTIVE + VERB</td><td>0</td><td>11</td><td>6</td><td>2</td><td>0</td><td>5</td><td>24</td></tr>
<tr><td>NOUN + VERB</td><td>0</td><td>1</td><td>5</td><td>0</td><td>0</td><td>2</td><td>8</td></tr>
<tr><td colspan="2">PARTICIPLE FUNCTIONS EXCLUSIVELY AS A NOUN</td><td>9</td><td>3</td><td>1</td><td>1</td><td>1</td><td>2</td><td>17</td></tr>
<tr><td colspan="9">16.2% of all participles fulfill the "intermediate" function in EBH
6.1% of all participles fulfill the "intermediate" function in LBH</td></tr>
</table>

[2]Even Shoshan quotes the twelfth century writer Ibn Ezra as using this term; this is the earliest reference to the term that I could find.

2.3.2. Criteria for Classification

In Table 2 are counted only those participles that are not lexicalized as nouns or adjectives. In the cases of "noun + verb" or "adjective + verb" the problem does not arise; clearly, even if the given participle has a lexicalized version, in the examples under consideration it is not used in that capacity. In those cases where the participle is used as a noun exclusively, I applied the following procedure: Using Mandelkern's concordance, I looked up all the occurrences of that participle in the entire Old Testament (in addition to its occurrences in the surveyed chapters). I checked to see, first of all, whether the verb exists as a perfect and imperfect. This assured me that it is at least true that the form under investigation CAN appear as a verb. Further, I checked if the participle ever appears in a context where it must be interpreted as a lexicalized noun rather than a participle. One feature that would make the form a lexicalized noun is indefiniteness. As we shall see in the section on relative clauses below, a participle will appear as a relative clause with only agreement in definiteness with the head and with no relativizer. In the great majority of cases, the head and the participle will be definite. Relevant to our discussion is the definite participle that constitutes a HEADLESS relative, as in the following examples (*ha-* is the definite marker):

ho^{w}*y*	*hå'omərī*^{y}*m*	*låra'*	*ṭo*^{w}*ƀ*
alas	the sayPAR-PL	to the bad	good

'alas, those who refer to evil as "good"'

However, when a single participle appears with no definite marker, there is less of a chance of it being a headless relative. Then it could be a lexicalized noun.

Next the question arises of the participle's place in the sentence. In MnH one can use an indefinite, non-lexicalized participle as the subject, but mostly not as a direct object. For example:

roked	*exad*	*patax*	*bešira*
dancePAR	one	opened	in singing

'some dancer started singing', 'a certain dancer (dancing person) started singing'

**etmol*	*pagašti*	*roked*	*exad*
yesterday	I met	dancePAR	one

'yesterday I met some dancer (a certain dancer)'

The quantifier 'one' is here used in the capacity of a determiner, 'some' or 'a certain'. Without this determiner, the participle could not appear even as a subject. So if the participle under investigation never appears as a direct object in such a situation, there is at least no indication that it IS lexicalized as a noun.

A further criterion, illustrated in the above example, is whether the participle has a competing form where the root is cast in a clearly nominal pattern which does not belong to the verbal system at all. Thus 'a dancer' is *rakdan* in MnH; there is no need for another noun with the same meaning, and so the participle, *roked*, is not lexicalized.

One last indication, though certainly not a conclusive one by itself, is if the participle appears coordinated with a "real" noun or as part of a list of such nouns. This means that it functions as a noun at least in the given sentence. If in addition it appears as an indefinite direct object, then the weight of the evidence is for its classification as a lexicalized noun. An example is *yo*^{w}*neq*, discussed immediately below.

This test procedure is not fool-proof, of course. It is possible, for example, that a native speaker could have provided a lexicalized-participle example with ease, although no such example happens to appear in the Bible. Still, if all the occurrences of a given participle seem to be verbal (or, more accurately, semi-verbal), then that participle belongs in the counting.

As it turned out, I found reason enough to delete from my list only one participle, *yo*^{w}*neq* (suckPAR) 'baby'. It does not appear in a clearly verbal function, and it does appear as an indefinite direct object AND as part of a list in a number of cases. For example:

miḥuʷṣ	*təsakkel*	*ḥereb*	...	*gam*	*bāḥuʷr*	*gam*	*bətuʷlāh*
from without	will bereave	sword	...	also	young man	also	virgin

yoʷneq	*'im*	*'iʸš*	*śeʸbāh*	(Deuteronomy 32.25)
suckPAR	with	man of	old age	

'a foreign sword will bereave a young man and a young woman, a baby and an old man'

2.3.3. What the Data Show

Now to the discussion of the "intermediate" form itself. This status of the participle has, of course, long been recognized. Bergsträsser (1926:425) mentions that the participle may convey a meaning which is between that of a state and that of a recurring action. Gesenius (1855:section 135) and the Encyclopaedia Judaica (1971, vol. 16:1577) say much the same thing. Blake (1951: 28-30) demonstrates the same point with a catalog of examples with little analysis or conclusions drawn. Givón (1977:209) refers to the fact that in nominal-genitive constructions, the participle is ambiguous, interpretable as either a verb followed by a direct object or as the "possessed" member in a possessive construction.

An example which struck me as an excellent demonstration of a noun + verb form is the following NP from EBH (although not taken from the texts I surveyed):

halwiyyim	*məšārətey*	*'otiʸ*	(Jeremiah 33.22)
the Levites	servePAR of	ACC-I	

'the Levites my servants / who serve me'

Here is a construct (a possessive construction), where the possessed is a participle. It takes the typical form of possessed plural masculine nouns: final *m* does not appear (the form of the word not in a possessive construction is *məšarətiʸm*), and rather than the *i*, *ey* appears. However, the possessor pronoun takes the accusative form (*'otiʸ*, 'ACC-I'), as though the participle preceding it were a transitive verb.

It should be stressed that normally the second member of the possessive construction of the type used here, be it a pronoun or a noun, does not take the accusative form. Hence, the form of the participle in the above example is accounted for only by the participle being taken as a noun, while the form of the possessor following it is accounted for only by the participle being taken as a verb.

Like nouns, participles can take *kɔl*, 'all':

lāken	*kɔl*	*horeg*	*qayin*	*šib'ātayim*	*yuqqām*	(Gn.4.15)
therefore	all	killPAR of	Cain	sevenfold	will be taken revenge on	

'therefore, whoever kills Cain, vengeance shall be taken on him sevenfold'

So much for the noun + verb usage. As for the adjectival participle (adjective + verb), an example is:

yəhuʷdāh	*w yiśrā'el*	*rabbiʸm*	*kaḥoʷl*	(I R.4.20)
Judah	and Israel	multiplyPAR	like sand	

'Judah and Israel are many like the sand'

rabbiʸm is an adjective, 'many', but it is also the participle of the verb which means 'to multiply'.

In the EBH texts, 16.2% of the participles fulfill such double function; in the LBH texts, 6.1% of the participles do. The trend then is for the intermediate function to decrease. I shall show that this trend continued into MH and MnH; polarization of the functions occurred, until in MnH every participle is clearly either verbal or nominal, and in fact, within the nominal category, every participle is either a noun or an adjective.

In the following sections I shall examine the use of the participle in various constructions. The peculiar nature of the participle, as explained above, gives rise to some special characteristics in these constructions. The first such construction is an equivalent of the adverbial clause, which I termed here the circumstantial adverbial.

2.4. Circumstantial Adverbials

These constructions describe the circumstances under which an action or event took place. Driver (1892:166) mentions these constructions as ones in which the participle appears, but says nothing about the concomitant syntactic phenomena discussed below. Givón too mentions the adverbial use of the participle but does not dwell on it (see, for example, Givón (1977:216)). Circumstantial adverbials are conjunct sentences that could be paraphrased as beginning with phrases such as "and all that time ...", "and at the same time ...", or, if the sentence is the first member in the conjunction, with "at the same time that ...", "when ...", "while ...". In BH, however, they are not marked with such adverbials; rather, they simply appear as conjuncts. I am using the term "circumstantial adverbials" so as to exclude sentences like conditionals and reason adverbials, which have subordinating conjunctions like 'because' and 'if'.

Examples:

uƀe^{y}t	*šɛmɛš*	*qoṣəri^{y}m*	*qəṣi^{y}r*	*ḥiṭṭi^{y}m*	*bå'emɛq*
and Beth	Shemesh	harvestPAR	harvest of	wheat	in the valley

wayyiśə'u^{w}	*'ɛŧ*	*'e^{y}ne^{y}hɛm*	*wayyirə'u^{w}*	*'ɛŧ*	*hå'åro^{w}n* (I S.6.13)
and they lifted	ACC	their eyes	and they saw	ACC	the ark

'as the people of Beth Shemesh were harvesting wheat in the valley, they looked up and saw the ark'

(The first conjunct is a circumstantial adverbial.)

wayyă'ălu^{w}	*kɔl*	*hå'åm*	*'aḥărå^{y}w*	*wəhå'åm*	*məhalləli^{y}m*
and came up	all	the people	after him	and the people	pipePAR

baḥălili^{y}m	(I R.1.40)
in pipes	

'and all the people followed him playing pipes'

(The second conjunct is a circumstantial adverbial.)

wayyo'mɛr	*li^{y}*	*hammɛlɛk*	*wəhaššeǥål*	*yo^{w}šɛƀɛŧ*	*'ɛṣlo^{w}*	(Neh.2.6)
and said	to me	the king	and the queen	sitPAR	with him ...	

'and the king said to me, while the queen was sitting next to him ...'

(The second conjunct is a circumstantial adverbial.)

mi^{y}	*zo'ŧ*	*'olå^{h}*	*min*	*hammiđbår*	*miŧrappɛqɛŧ*	*'al*	*dođåh*	(Cant.8.5)
who	this	come upPAR	from	the desert	leanPAR	on	her lover	

'who is this coming up from the desert, leaning on her lover?'

(No syntactic marker appears for the circumstantial adverbial. The other examples had the conjunction *wə* 'and' between the adverbial and the other clause.)

In all these cases it is only the appearance of the participle which indicates that the adverbial and the tensed verb do not express a sequence of events. This effect of the participle is perhaps similar to the effect of the present participle in English, in sentences like *How could I concentrate with John laughing hysterically all the time?* Of course, here the preposition *with* signals the adverbial status of the following clause, but the form of the verb is also such a signal. In BH, it is quite sufficient to use a participle in order to show the adverbial status of a sentence; the element joining it to the other sentence is a coordinating conjunction, or it may appear without such a joining element altogether.

Not surprisingly, replacing the participle with a tensed verb creates a conjunction of sentences expressing a sequence of events. For example, if we replace the participle in the first quotation above with a verb in the perfect (preceding time reference), *qåṣəru*^{w} 'harvested', the meaning of the sentence would be, 'the people of Beth Shemesh harvested in the valley, and (afterwards) they looked up and saw the ark'.

The last row in Table 3 lists the cases where the circumstantial adverbials are marked, as in MnH, with the typical marker *kəše-* 'when' and with *'ad* here meaning 'when' (a meaning it has since iost).

TABLE 3.
Circumstantial Adverbials

<table>
<tr><th colspan="3">BOOK</th><th>GN</th><th>I S</th><th>I R</th><th>CANT</th><th>ECCL</th><th>NEH</th><th>TOTAL</th></tr>
<tr><td rowspan="3">SUBORDINATION WITHOUT A SUBORDINATING MARKER</td><td rowspan="2">ADVERBIAL CONJUNCTION (WITH 'AND')</td><td>FIRST MEMBER</td><td>0</td><td>3</td><td>3</td><td>0</td><td>0</td><td>0</td><td>6</td></tr>
<tr><td>SECOND MEMBER</td><td>0</td><td>14</td><td>13</td><td>0</td><td>0</td><td>8</td><td>35</td></tr>
<tr><td colspan="2">ADVERBIAL WITH NO SYNTACTIC MARKER</td><td>1</td><td>2</td><td>2</td><td>2</td><td>0</td><td>0</td><td>7</td></tr>
<tr><td colspan="3">SUBORDINATION WITH A MARKER ('WHEN' ETC.)</td><td>0</td><td>0</td><td>0</td><td>0</td><td>1</td><td>1</td><td>2</td></tr>
</table>

The decline in the number of circumstantial adverbials is clear. As the participle approaches the status of a regular, tensed verb, the danger increases of circumstantial adverbials being perceived as events in sequence with the main verb. Therefore, the use of such adverbials decreases, from 38 in EBH (26.8% of all EBH participles) to 10 in LBH (6.7% of all LBH participles). At the same time, other devices are adopted for the purpose of introducing circumstantial adverbials, i.e. special adverbs like *kəše-* 'when'.

The above analysis predicts that circumstantial adverbials with tensed verbs are impossible, and indeed this is so. Sentences like the following appear at first to be counter-examples:

ha'ap	*'umnåm*	*'eled*	*wa'ăni*^{y}	*zåqanti*^{y}	(Gn.18.13)
INTERROGATIVE even	really	I will give birth	and I	grew old	

'will I give birth after (now that) I have grown old?'

However, notice that the second verb does not depend on the first for time reference. There IS a sequence of events here: first, the growing old, and then the possibility of giving birth. Not surprisingly, the second clause cannot begin with 'and at the same time'; no circumstantial adverbial is present.

2.5. Relative Clauses with Participles

2.5.1. The Relativizer

Another construction where the appearance of the participle requires a special examination is the relative clause. In BH, the relativizer for relatives with verbs in the perfect or the imperfect is *'ăšɛr* 'that', alternating in many cases in LBH with the prefix *šɛ-*. There are various opinions about the relationship between the two relativizers. Some see *šɛ-* as derived from *'ăšɛr*; others see the latter as derived from the former (see Peretz (1967:28-29) for a review of these approaches). But the position generally accepted is that the two are etymologically unrelated (see Rabin (1960:13-14, 1972:21-22); Peretz (1967:128-30)). It appears that *šɛ-* was used in Northern Israel, while *'ăšɛr* was used in the literary dialect of the south, which was the official dialect of the kingdom in EBH time, as I explained above. This is why *'ăšɛr* is prevalent in EBH. The cases of *šɛ-* are those in which the spoken dialect of the writer, probably a Northern-Israelite, manifests itself. In LBH, the use of *šɛ-* increases, apparently due to the decline of the official dialect after the destruction of the first temple in Jerusalem by Babylonia and the exile of the upper classes to Babylonia (Peretz 1967: 127). Hence, the increase in *šɛ-* in itself is not a matter of linguistic development.

Now to the relativizer in relatives with participles. In these cases there are two possibilities: depending on the particular sentence, either *'ăšɛr* / *šɛ-* will appear, or the participle will merely agree with the head noun. Let us examine the two possibilities in greater detail.

If the subject is relativized on, then in most cases no relativizer appears. Rather, agreement in definiteness with the head appears on the participle (in addition to the agreement in gender and number and lack of agreement in person, as is always the case with participles, in or out of relative clauses). Such agreement is identical with the agreement that adjectives show.

hakkənaʿăni^{y}	*hayyošeƀ*	*båʿi^{y}r*	(I R.9.16)
the Canaanite	the dwellPAR	in the city	

'the Canaanites who dwell in the city'

As we shall see below (Table 5), clauses with participles are SVO ordered. Thus, when the subject is deleted in relativization as in the example above, the participle follows the head immediately. However, sometimes other matter (negator or copula) appears in initial position, i.e. between the head and the participle, or the subject relativized on IS represented (by a pronoun). In such cases, the definiteness agreement never appears; rather *'ăšɛr* always appears.

'ĕlohe^{y}kɛm	*'ăšɛr*	*hu'*	*mo^{w}šiaʿ*	*låkɛm*	(I S.10.19)
your God	that	he	savePAR	to you	

'your God who saves you' / 'your God who is the one who saves you'

When a non-subject is relativized on, *'ăšɛr* or *šɛ-* is mandatory:

kɔl	*ʿămåli^{y}*	*šɛ'ăni^{y}*	*ʿåmel*	(Eccl.2.18)
all	my toil	that I	toilPAR	

'all the work that I do'

Such cases are counted in the row marked "Otherwise Conditioned" in the table below.

And finally, sometimes the subject is relativized on, nothing appears between the head and the participle, and yet the relativizer *'ăšɛr* or *šɛ-* appears (row marked "Not Otherwise Conditioned" in Table 4):

hå'ezo^{w}ƀ	*'ăšɛr*	*yoṣe'*	*baqqi^{y}r*	(I R.5.13)
the hyssop	that	go outPAR	in the wall	

'the hyssop that grows on the wall'

Following is a most interesting example:

kadågi^{y}*m*	*šɛnnɛ'ĕḥåzi*^{y}*m*	*bimṣo*^{w}*dåh*	*rå'åh*	*wəkaṣṣippŏri*^{y}*m*
like the fish	that are caughtPAR	in net	bad	and like the birds

hå'ăḥuzzo^{w}*t*	*bappåḥ*	(Eccl.9.12)
the are caughtPAR	in the snare	

'like the fish that are caught in an evil net and like the birds that are caught in a snare'

Here we have two relatives, both on subjects, but one has *šɛ-*, the other has agreement.

TABLE 4.
Relative Clauses with Participles

<table>
<tr><td colspan="3">BOOK</td><td>GN</td><td>I S</td><td>I R</td><td>CANT</td><td>ECCL</td><td>NEH</td><td>TOTAL</td></tr>
<tr><td rowspan="4">RELATIVES ON SUBJECT</td><td colspan="2">BY AGREEMENT</td><td>6
(85.7)</td><td>12
(80)</td><td>14
(82.4)</td><td>5
(100)</td><td>5
(27.8)</td><td>13
(54.2)</td><td>55
(64)</td></tr>
<tr><td rowspan="2">WITH
'ăšɛr / šɛ-</td><td>OTHERWISE CONDITIONED</td><td>0
(0)</td><td>1
(6.6)</td><td>1
(5.9)</td><td>0
(0)</td><td>3
(16.6)</td><td>1
(4.2)</td><td>6
(7)</td></tr>
<tr><td>NOT OTHERWISE CONDITIONED</td><td>0
(0)</td><td>0
(0)</td><td>1
(5.9)</td><td>0
(0)</td><td>2
(11.1)</td><td>3
(12.5)</td><td>6
(7)</td></tr>
<tr><td colspan="2">TOTAL RELATIVES ON SUBJECT</td><td>6
(85.7)</td><td>13
(86.6)</td><td>16
(94.1)</td><td>5
(100)</td><td>10
(55.6)</td><td>17
(70.8)</td><td>67
(78)</td></tr>
<tr><td colspan="3">RELATIVES ON NON-SUBJECT
(ALWAYS WITH 'ăšɛr / šɛ-)</td><td>1
(14.3)</td><td>2
(13.3)</td><td>1
(5.9)</td><td>0
(0)</td><td>8
(44.4)</td><td>7
(29.2)</td><td>19
(22)</td></tr>
<tr><td colspan="3">TOTAL RELATIVES</td><td>7</td><td>15</td><td>17</td><td>5</td><td>18</td><td>24</td><td>86</td></tr>
</table>

(In parentheses: percentage out of total relatives for that book, as in bottom row)

An examination of the table, especially the use of *'ăšɛr / šɛ-*, shows that the participle is very much like an adjective. In fact, in those cases where it is close to an NP head, its adjective quality must apparently have been predominant for the speakers who treated it not like the predicate of a relative clause, which requires *'ăšɛr*, but rather like an attributive adjective, which takes agreement with the head. Other than the participle, no form of the verb takes agreement rather than *'ăšɛr* when it appears in a relative clause modifying a head noun. The fact that participles can take agreement indicates that sometimes (when adjacent to the head) they are perceived as adjective-like.

If participles in relatives are very much like adjectives, why, then, are there all those cases when such relatives DO receive *'ăšɛr / šɛ-* ? Because attributive adjectives are never distant from their heads, in BH as well as in MnH. As far as I can see, only intensifiers and negators are allowed between the head and the adjective. Here are MnH examples, which are representative of BH too:

iša	*meod*	*xaxama*
woman	very	wise

'a very wise woman'

iša	*lo*	*xaxama*
woman	not	wise

'an unwise woman'

Other intervening matter is forbidden:

**iša*	*mirušalayim*	*xaxama*	
woman	from Jerusalem	wise	'a wise woman from Jerusalem'

But participles, after all, are not quite identical with adjectives. When they appear in a position where adjectives cannot appear, e.g. when a lower subject intervenes between the participle and the head, they cannot be equated with adjectives. Furthermore, even if the speakers did equate them with adjectives, the definiteness-agreement mechanism did not (and still does not) operate over intervening matter.

In such cases, one of two developments is possible: either agreement WILL be extended, and adjectives, as well as participles, will begin to appear removed from their heads ("participle is adjective" conception prevails), or even those participles adjacent to heads will stop taking agreement and start taking *šɛ-* ("participle is verb" conception prevails). Now consider the figures. The percentage of subject relatives which, despite having nothing between the head and the participle, display *'ăšɛr* or *šɛ-* is, in the order of the books in the table 0%, 0%, 5.8%, 0%, 11.1%, 12.5%. Consider also that MnH has all but completed the shift to *šɛ-* with all relatives, and the direction of development matches our other findings: the participle in relatives becomes a full-fledged verb.

2.5.2. What Sentence Element Is Relativized on?

It is evident from the table that most relatives with participles are subject relatives. Is this true for all relatives in BH? Following is the situation in the ten chapters surveyed in I Kings:

TABLE 5.
Non-Participle Relatives

	RELATIVE ON SUBJECT	RELATIVE ON NON-SUBJECT
Relative has perfect	18	54
Relative has imperfect	4	13
Relative is a nominal sentence (has no tense)	2	3
Relative is *'ăšɛr* + PP (has no tense)	31	–

The third row refers to relatives with predicate nominals, like

*hå'iššå^h^* *'ăšɛr* *bənåh* *haḥay* (I R.3.26)
the woman that her son the livePAR
'the woman whose son was the living one'

and the fourth row refers to relatives like

hɛḥåcer *'ăšɛr* *lipney* *bey^y^t* *'ădonåy* (I R.8.64)
the yard that in front of the house of God
'the yard in front of the house of God'

In all, then, there are 55 subject relatives and 70 non-subject relatives. However, the last two rows refer to relatives that, like those with participles, have no tense and must receive their time-reference from the context. They must then be counted with the participle relatives, and like the latter, they display an overwhelming tendency towards being subject relatives. The ratio for tensed relatives is thus 22 subject relatives as against 67 non-subject relatives. The conclusion of this examination of I Kings is, then, that TENSED relatives display the reverse tendency to that of non-tensed ones: they are mostly non-subject relatives.

It is seen that the participles with their tendency to appear in subject relatives, took away much of the burden otherwise carried by tensed verbs. Recall that the time reference of the participles can be exactly that of tensed verbs; thus, in a relative referenced to, say, preceding time, the speaker may use the perfect, or he may use the participle and provide a time-reference clue in the context as in Table 1. The crucial question is, why is it that for subject relatives the speaker usually selects the participle, rather than a tensed verb?

Perhaps this is the result of a tendency to economize in the complexity of the NP: where an adjective would perform the same task as a relative clause, the adjective is preferred. If this principle or a similar one is indeed operating in the text, then the facts are explained. Take the following NP (a MnH example, but valid for BH as well):

haiš *ašer* *šavar* *kos*
the man that broke glass
'the man who broke a glass'

If a participle were inserted instead of the tensed verb, agreement could be assigned to it, and the construction would look just like a noun + relative NP, as I explained above. Thus greater economy in the complexity of the NP would be achieved. The resulting NP might be,

haiš *šover* *hakos*
the man breakPAR of the glass
'the man (who is) the breaker of the glass'

This might explain why subject relatives tend to use participles.

Now suppose that the object in the phrase 'the man who broke a glass' above is relativized on and deleted (a resumptive pronoun may be inserted in its place). Here a relative clause cannot be avoided because the verb is not adjacent to the head; even with a participle, *'ăšer* is obligatory. This explains why non-subject relatives do not display the tendency to use the participle.

2.6. Subject Position

I now turn to the examination of another construction, the sentence, as affected by the participle. In particular, I will examine subject position.

TABLE 6.
Subject Position

BOOK	GN	I S	I R	CANT	ECCL	NEH	TOTAL
SUBJECT IS NOT SENTENCE INITIAL[3]	1	5	0	1	9	1	17
TOTAL PARTICIPLES IN BOOK (AS IN TABLE 1)	22	59	61	19	55	75	291

Not much change is shown here. With tensed verbs, unmarked BH word order is VSO, but it is SVO with participles. This is because the participle, as a nominal element, follows the subject, just as a regular predicate nominal would.[4] The few cases where the participle precedes the subject can most probably be attributed to multiple analysis, i.e. this is where the first signs of the

[3]There may be some extraneous reason for the subject not being sentence initial, e.g. a sentence-initial adverb. Such cases are not counted in this table.

[4]This fact is recognized in the literature. See, for example, Driver (1892:167), and Bendavid (1967:807-808).

participle as a verb show up. However, as we shall see in the discussion of MnH, it is NOT the case that when the participle was unequivocally reanalyzed as a verb, it took initial position; rather, by that time the word order in the language had changed to SVO, and so the participle retained second position.

It is clear, then, that I regard the nominal aspect of the participle as the main reason for the preponderance of SVO order in sentences with participles; I claim that the participle functions as a predicate nominal, and predicate nominals follow the subject in Hebrew, Biblical, Mishnaic, and Modern. However, Givón (1977:211) proposes another reason: since, unlike other verbs, the participle does not display person agreement with the subject, the subject cannot be ellipted. At least a subject pronoun is required, and subject pronouns normally appear sentence-initially. Therefore the word order associated with the participle. My only hesitation regarding this explanation is that it would seem to predict VSO order when a FULL noun is present as subject, which is not the case. In fact such a sentence sounds highly awkward for BH. To use an example quoted above, let us try to reverse the subject and the participle in it.

wayyo'mɛr	*li*^{y}	*hammɛlɛꝁ*	*wəhaššeǥå̊l*	*yo*^{w}*šɛƀɛŧ*	*'ɛṣlo*^{w}	...	(Neh.2.6)
and said	to me	the king	and the queen	sitPAR	with him ...		

'and the king said to me, while the queen was sitting next to him ...'

S-V reversed:

wayyo'mɛr	*li*^{y}	*hammɛlɛꝁ*	*wəyo*^{w}*šɛƀɛŧ*	*haššeǥal*	*'ɛṣlo*^{w}	...
and said	to me	the king	and sitPAR	the queen	with him ...	

This last sentence, though not "wrong", sounds very foreign to BH style. I therefore believe that viewing the participle predicate as a predicate nominal explains the SVO order associated with it.

2.7. The Construction *hå̊yå̊*^{h} + Participle

2.7.1. The Various Functions of *hå̊yå̊*^{h} and the Discussion in the Literature

The last construction I will examine with respect to the behavior of the participle in it is the sentence with *hå̊yå̊*^{h} 'be'. As is customary in Hebrew, I am using the past third person masculine singular form of the verb as the base form. The root is *h-y-y*, and the verb is sometimes referred to by its root in the literature.

The categories in the following table are self explanatory.

TABLE 7.
The Function of *hå̊yå̊*^{h}

BOOK	GN	I S	I R	CANT	ECCL	NEH	TOTAL
FUNCTIONS AS A COPULA	3	1	0	0	0	1	5
PROVIDES TIME REFERENCE TO PAR	0	0	0	0	0	5	5
IMPARTS HABITUAL MEANING	0	0	0	0	0	0	0
IMPARTS CONTINUOUS MEANING	0	0	0	0	0	0	0
IMPARTS ITERATIVE MEANING	0	0	0	0	0	3	3

In MnH *hå̊yå̊*^{h} is either a copula or an auxiliary. In the latter capacity it can impart the meaning of repeated (perhaps also habitual and continuous) action (further details in the discussion of MnH below). In BH, *håyå*^{h} is usually a copula, and is used with nominals. It does not appear with tensed verbs. As the table shows, however, it does appear with participles.

In the literature the discussion of this construction is usually general and rather brief. Bergsträsser (1926:425) says that *håyå*^{h} before a participle shows that a certain content, expressible with a participle, happened in the past. Driver (1892:169) describes the construction as typically showing the background to some other action. He explains that *håyå*^{h} + participle is more prevalent in LBH than in EBH because of the "decadence" of the language, which, having lost some of its other means of expressing that content, resorts to innovations (decadent ones, no doubt) like this construction. The decadence issue notwithstanding, I find that my conclusions, expressed below, are not contrary to Driver's.

Blake (1951:30) claims that the *håyå*^{h} + participle is a construction expressing past progressive, past passive, and future passive. The first of the list is rather close to my own findings. However, for the other two he quotes examples with a passive participle, such as

ki^{y}	*muli*^{y}*m*	*håyu*^{w}	*kɔl*	*hå'åm*	*håyyoṣə'i*^{y}*m*	(Joshua 5.5)
because	circumcise-PASSIVE-PAR	were	all	the nation	the leavePAR	

'because all the people who left were circumcised'

Here the passivity is inherent in the participle and has nothing to do with the *håyå*^{h}. We are left, then, with the first of Blake's list of three usages of the construction.

Segal (1909:52) is very close to Blake in his description. He says that the *håyå*^{h} + participle conveys the meaning of an iterative action or an action which continues along some stretch of time.

Segal adds a very interesting point. Nehemiah, he says, in which most of LBH *håyå*^{h} + participle constructions are found (all of them in my texts), was intended for personal use as a book of memoirs, and was therefore written in a colloquial dialect with no attempt to imitate the literary tradition of EBH. By the time the Mishnah was written, that literary tradition had stopped being used altogether. Therefore, in Nehemiah and in MH the use of *håyå*^{h} + participle increases as compared with EBH. As we shall see in the next chapter, many writers regard MH as an older local dialect which surfaced with the demise of the official, literary dialect of EBH, and so Segal's opinion is supported.

An equally interesting point in Segal's discussion is his convincing demonstration (pp. 52-53) that although Aramaic was the official language of the administration in LBH times, still, contrary to other scholars' opinions, Aramaic influence did not cause the increase in *håyå*^{h} + participle, but at most accelerated it. His most convincing argument is that, although Aramaic has the equivalent of *håyå*^{h} followed by past and future as well as by participles, Hebrew has only the latter.

2.7.2. Analysis of the Data

I move on now to the discussion of the exact nature of the construction in the text, first in EBH and then in LBH. Following are the cases of this construction in EBH.

wihyi^{y}*ŧɛm*	*ke'lohi*^{y}*m*	*yodə'e*^{y}	*ṭo*^{w}*ƀ*	*wårå'*	(Gn.3.5)
and youPL will be	like God	knowPAR-PL of	good	and evil	

'and you will be like God, knowers of good and evil' / 'and you will know good and evil like God'

nå'	*wånåđ*	*tihyɛ*^{h}	*bå'årɛṣ*	(Gn.4.12)
travelPAR	and wanderPAR	you will be	in the land	

'you will be a traveler and a wanderer in the land'

wəhåyi^{y}*ŧi*^{y}	*nå'*	*wånåđ*	*bå'årɛṣ*	(Gn.4.14)
and I will be	travelPAR	and wanderPAR	in the land	

'and I will be a traveler and a wanderer in the land'

wayəhi^{y} *kəmaḥări^{y}š* (I S.10.27)
and he was like keep quietPAR
'and he was like one who keeps quiet' / 'he remained silent'

In all of these, the participle conveys a general time/habitual meaning, which is the closest that participles can get to nominals. In fact, the last participle even has a preposition *kə* 'like', which further shows its nominal character. Serving as a copula, *håyå^{h}* is used here much as it would be used with nominals. As such, it provides the time reference of the sentence, and to the extent that the participles are construed as verbal, they receive their time reference from the *håyå^{h}*.

Now consider the cases of *håyå^{h}* + participle in LBH:

yåšaƀti^{y} *wå'ɛƀkɛ^{h}* *wå'ɛŧ'abbəlå^{h}* *yåmi^{y}m* *wå'ɛhi^{y}* *ṣåm* *umiŧpallel* (Neh.1.4)
I sat and I cried and I lamented days and I was fastPAR and prayPAR
'I sat and cried and lamented for days and I fasted and prayed'

wå'eṣ'å^{h} *ƀša'ar* *haggay'* ... *wå'ɛhi^{y}* *šoƀer*
and I went out in the gate of the valley ... and I was lookPAR

bəḥo^{w}moŧ *yəru^{w}šålaim* (Neh.2.13)
in the walls of Jerusalem

'and I went out through the Valley Gate ... and I surveyed the walls of Jerusalem'

wå'ɛhi^{y} *'olɛ^{h}* *ƀannaḥal* *laylå^{h}* *wå'ɛhi^{y}* *šoƀer* *baḥo^{w}må^{h}*
and I was ascendPAR in the valley night and I was lookPAR in the wall

wå'åšu^{w}ƀ *wå'åƀo^{w}'* *bəša'ar* *haggay'* *wå'åšu^{w}ƀ* (Neh.2.15)
and I returned and I came in the gate of the valley and I returned

'and I went up the valley at night and I surveyed the wall and returned, and I entered through the Valley Gate and returned'

wəhannŧi^{y}ni^{y}m *håyu^{w}* *yošƀi^{y}m* *bå'oᵽɛl* (Neh.3.26)
and the Netinim were dwellPAR-PL in the hill
'and the Netinim dwelt on the hill'

uləyɛŧɛr *hannəƀi^{y}'i^{y}m* *'ăšɛr* *håyu^{w}* *məyårə'i^{y}m* *'o^{w}ŧi^{y}* (Neh.6.14)
and to the rest of the prophets that were make afraidPAR me
'and to the rest of the prophets who were (trying to) make me afraid'

gam *ṭo^{w}ƀoŧå^{y}w* *håyu^{w}* *'omәri^{y}m* *ləᵽånay* *uđəƀåray* *håyu^{w}*
also his praise were sayPAR-PL before me and my words were

mo^{w}ṣi^{y}'i^{y}m *lo^{w}* (Neh.6.19)
take outPAR-PL to him

'also, they praised him to me and reported my words to him'

As I mentioned above (see 2.7.1), Segal (1909) concludes that the *håyå^{h}* + participle construction, which is exemplified above, is native to Hebrew, and although it is prevalent in Aramaic, it was not borrowed from Aramaic into Hebrew. However, Aramaic influence might have helped the development of the construction in Hebrew.

Consider the six LBH examples. The participles in the first three are different than those in EBH in that they cannot be construed as general/habitual. They all come in a series of verbs, of which the ones preceding or following the participles are tensed verbs (with suffix or prefix morphology).

Clearly, all the verbs relate a sequence of events, none of which occurred while another was in progress, none of which is more habitual or continuous or repeated than the others. This being the case, one cannot claim that the participle in these three cases is general/habitual and therefore nominal in some way; *håyå^h* therefore cannot be a copula. The participle here is a verb among other verbs, except that unlike tensed verbs it lacks a time reference inherent in its own morphology. The sole function left for the *håyå^h*, then, is to provide that time reference. This must be Gesenius' (1855:sec. 134) intention when he says that *håyå^h* + participle is sometimes used in BH for "periphrasis of the imperfect". He must mean that the construction is used instead of a regular verb in a series of verbs relating the story, NOT with a general/habitual or continuous import.

Now to the participles in the last three examples above. Here *håyå^h* indicates a repeated action, and also gives the time reference, as it does in the first three examples.

Thus, in all of the six examples, the *håyå^h* can be regarded as an AUXILIARY VERB. In Nehemiah, then, the development of the participle towards becoming a regular, tensed verb is seen in the fact that participles receive their time reference by inference (40.3%–an unusually high number) and by auxiliary verb, both of which ways are typically verbal (inference, of course, is typically verbal in that it is the precursor of inherent tense, as I explained above).

2.7.3. The Origin of *håyå^h* as the only Auxiliary Verb in Hebrew

An interesting reanalysis is seen here. The *håyå^h* before a participle serves a double function in EBH, namely, it is a copula and a time referencing clue at the same time. In LBH, as the participle begins to become more and more verb-like, the *håyå^h* which precedes it in such constructions cannot fulfill such double function any more. However, the construction does not fall out of use. Rather, it is re-interpreted according to the nature of the participle following it, and the *håyå^h* accepts the role of an auxiliary verb. A telling fact is that in BH, MH and MnH, *håyå^h* + participle is the only construction where one can point to an auxiliary verb. WE SEE NOW THAT THE ORIGIN OF THIS RATHER UNUSUAL CONSTRUCTION FOR HEBREW IS THE "INTERMEDIATE" NATURE OF THE EBH PARTICIPLE and the consequent development that that participle underwent.

2.8. Negation

2.8.1. The Data

In BH, as well as in MH and in MnH, the negator *lo'* 'not' is used for tensed verbs, while the negator *'e^{y}n* 'there is not' is used for nouns. It would therefore be interesting to see how the participle is negated. In the chapters that I analyzed for the previous sections, very little negation of the participle is found. I therefore turned to Mandelkern's concordance for references to every negated participle in the entire six books from which I used chapters for the previous sections.

The results of the count are indeed striking. In the entire six books, I did not find a single case of *lo'* negating a participle. I should mention that in MnH *lo* (the descendant of the BH *lo'*), which is the verbal negator, functions almost universally for negation of the participle in colloquial use. In written use both appear, with *'e^{y}n* having a more formal nature. The numbers for BH are in Table 8.

TABLE 8.
Negation of the Participle

BOOK	GN	I S	I R	CANT	ECCL	NEH	TOTAL
PARTICIPLES NEGATED WITH *'e^{y}n*	7	10	3	0	11	3	34
PARTICIPLES NEGATED WITH *lo'*	0	0	0	0	0	0	0

The nominal negation of the participle was briefly noted by some writers. The Encyclopaedia Judaica (1971, vol. 16, 1577) remarks that the participle is negated by *'e*^{y}*n* in BH. Segal (1909: 45) while discussing negation in MH does cite a few examples of participles negated with *lo'* in BH (in books other than the ones I dealt with), but it is clear from his discussion that these are exceptions to the rule; and Weiss too (1867:88) calls this usage of *lo'* + participle "the strange way" of negating the participle as compared to *'e*^{y}*n* + participle, which is the normal way. My point is, of course, that the few occurrences of *lo'* + participle, rather than being "strange", are harbingers of the change that the participle will undergo towards becoming a verbal form.

These facts show also that the origin of the participle as a nominal form is strongly felt in BH. Even when, in LBH, the participle takes on verbal qualities, its negation is that of a noun. That negator is one of the last noun qualities to be lost by the participle.

2.8.2. The Principle Underlying Propensity and Reluctance to Change

The reason for this reluctance on the part of users to change the negator ties in with other phenomena that we have seen, and allows us to reach a general principle: THE PARTICIPLE WAS SLOW TO CHANGE ITS APPEARANCE, its visible qualities. Its morphology, i.e. lack of person agreement, which gives the participle the appearance of a noun, never changed, even in MnH. Also, we have seen that *håyå*^{h}, which was necessary only for a participle that is semi-nominal, remained with the participle even when the participle became verbal and was reanalyzed as an auxiliary verb rather than jettisoned, although no other verbs in Hebrew (at any historical stage) take auxiliary verbs. And last we see that the nominal negator, another highly visible companion of the participle, is slow to change. Qualities that changed more quickly are the less obvious, the less visible ones. Thus, time reference by narrative or by inference are not visible in that they have no specific morphemes whose sole function it is to assign that reference, and so these ways of time reference are faster to change.

This concludes the discussion of BH. The definite development that is seen in the participle in the direction of becoming a full-fledged verb when used in its verbal capacity continues in MH, which is discussed in the next chapter. Then both BH and MH come together for the creation of MnH, and the state of the participle in that layer of the language is discussed in the last chapter.

3. MISHNAIC HEBREW

3.1. The Mishnah

3.1.1. Background

The following discussion uses as data the first ten chapters of Seder Nashim, or the order entitled 'Women'. The first ten chapters are concerned with the act of *yibbu*^{w}*m*, or 'levirate marriage'. References in the text give chapter and study numbers. Thus (3:4) refers to Chapter 3, Study 4.

The second gloss line below the quotations often attempts to do the impossible, i.e. explain the sometimes perplexingly terse Mishnaic law out of context and only partially quoted, with phrases irrelevant to my point left out. I thus beg the reader's indulgence and trust that the cryptic Hebrew in fact means what the second gloss line claims it to mean. The reader, of course, is not asked to accept my LINGUISTIC observations on faith; the linguistically relevant data are not omitted.

It is generally acknowledged today in the literature that, previous opinions notwithstanding, MH is not a learned and written Hebraization of Aramaic, but rather a living and spoken dialect, existent already in BH times, which became prevalent after the destruction of the first temple in Jerusalem and the exile of the people from the Land of Israel to Babylon (586 B.C.) (see the Encyclopaedia

Judaica (1971:vol. 16, 1590-91); Peretz (1967:24-28); Bendavid (1967:101-106, 153-56); Rabin (1960: 19-21; 1972:24-27)).

3.1.2. Tense in MH

The shift from a dual system of tense or aspect to a tripartite tense system begun in BH is, on the whole, completed in MH (see, for example, Rabin (1960:30)). Generally speaking, the past form–morphologically, the suffixed form–refers mainly to preceding time, the future form–the prefixed form–refers to consequent time, and the participle is used as a present tense form to refer to concurrent time with a few exceptions. Let us see a few examples. First, here are two examples of future used for consequent time:

'im	*hălåꝁå*^{h}	*nəqabbel*	*wə'im*	*lådi*^{y}*n*	*yeš*	*təšu*^{w}*ƀå*^{h}	(8:3)
if	a ruling	we will accept	and if	to discuss	there is	answer	

'if this is a ruling we will accept it, but if still debatable, we have a counter argument'

Clearly the speakers have not accepted anything yet; if told that what they heard is the ruling, THEN they will accept it, but obviously they have a different opinion.

'åmar	*rabbi*^{y}	*yəho*^{w}*šua'*	...	*wə'e*^{y}*n*	*li*^{y}	*ləpåreš*
said	Rabbi	Yehoshua	...	and there is not	to me	to explain

'åmar	*rabbi*^{y}	*'ăqi*^{y}*ƀå'*	*'ăni*^{y}	*'ăᵽåres*	(8:4)
said	Rabbi	Akiva	I	will explain	

'said Rabbi Yehoshua ... "I cannot explain (the reason for this ruling)." Said Rabbi Akiva, "I will explain (it)"'.

There is extensive use of the future for another purpose, the statement of law; whether that indicates that the shift to a tense system is not complete I shall discuss below.

Now here is an example of past tense referring to preceding time, and at the same time fulfilling the function of relating the narrative (reserved for the converted prefix form in EBH):

uma'ăśe^h	*bi*^{y}*ho*^{w}*šua'*	*ben*	*gamlå'*	*šeqqiddeš*	*'eŧ*	*martå'*
and occurrence	in Yehoshua	son of	Gamla	that betrothed	ACC	Martha

baŧ	*bayŧo*^{w}*s*	*umi*^{y}*nåhu*^{w}	*hammeleꝁ*	*lihyo*^{w}*t*
daughter of	Baytos	and appointed him	the king	to be

kohen	*gåđo*^{w}*l*	*uꝁnåsåh*	(6:4)
priest	big	and he took her	

'and it happened to Yehoshua, son of Gamla, that he betrothed Martha, the daughter of Baytos; then the king appointed him high priest, and (yet) he consummated the marriage'

(Martha was a widow; high priests cannot normally marry widows.) 'Betrothed', 'appointed', and 'consummated' took place in this order. Thus the past tense fulfills the narrative function.

I have exemplified the use of past and future; the use of the participle is, of course, the main concern of the rest of this chapter.

3.2. Time Reference

3.2.1. The Data

Let us examine the data concerning how the participle refers to time and see how the participle functions in the new system The categories in Table 9 below have the same meanings as in the counterpart table for BH.

TABLE 9.
Time Reference

TOTAL PARTICIPLES		252
TOTAL TIME-REFERENCED PARTICIPLES		250
HOW DOES THE PARTICIPLE REFER TO TIME? (IN PARENTHESES: % OF TOTAL TIME-REFERENCED PARTICIPLES)[5]	INFERENCE	0 (0)
	INDICATOR	5 (2)
	NARRATIVE	3 (1.2)
	UNBOUNDED	242 (96.8)
WHAT TIME DOES THE PARTICIPLE REFER TO? (IN PARENTHESES: % OF TIME-REFERENCED PARTICIPLES)	CONCURRENT	1 (0.4)
	PRECEDING (3 are also habitual/iterative)	6 (2.4)
	SUBSEQUENT	0 (0)
	GENERAL	243 (97.2)
THE PARTICIPLE IS USED FOR:	LAW	144 (59.3% of all general time participles)
	"SUCH AND SUCH SAYS"	32 (13.2% of all general time participles)
FUTURE USED FOR LAW		82 (92.1% of all futures)
TOTAL FUTURES		89
PAST USED FOR LAW		14
TOTAL VERB FORMS WITH TIME REFERENCE USED FOR LAW		240

3.2.2. Conclusions Regarding Time Reference

The participle obviously needs no external device to give it time reference; 96.8% of the participles that refer to time do so without such a device. At this point it is already possible to say that the very morphology of the verb is enough to make it interpretable as having general time reference. The row in the table may be called "inherent time reference" rather than "unbounded" (I have retained the previous designation to make the BH and MH tables easily comparable). An example of an inherent-reference participle is:

hameš	*‘ɛśre*^{h}	*nåši*^{y}*m*	*potəro*^{w}*t*	*ṣåro*^{w}*ŧe*^{y}*hɛn*
fifteen		women	exempt	their fellow wives

[5]Two participles have no time reference—see section 3.4.

min	*haḥăli*^{y}*ṣå*^{h}	*umin*	*hayyibbu*^{w}*m*	(1:1)
from	the shoe removal	and from	the levirate marriage	

'fifteen (categories of) women exempt their fellow wives ... from "shoe-removal" and from levirate marriage'[6]

Now to the other cases, where the indicator and the narrative give the participle its time reference. The "indicator" cases, all except one, are cases with *håyå*^{h}, which is an auxiliary (to be discussed separately below). As such it does carry the time reference. The other case of time by indicator is:

nimnə'u^{w}	*'o*^{w}*ŝi*^{y}*n*	(1:3)
they refrained	doPAR-PL	

'they refrained from doing'

'Refrained' gives time reference to the participle. This is one example where the participle does not have its own time reference, but accepts it from the environment. Keep in mind, however, that this is a very small percentage of the cases. Furthermore, such a construction normally has an infinitive instead of the participle. In six out of seven cases of 'refrained' which Kasowski (1967:vol. 3, 1146) cites, 'refrained' is followed by an infinitive, and only in one is it followed by the participle. Generally, then, the participle does have its inherent reference.

Now to the three cases where the narrative provides time reference. In all of them, the construction is an odd one.

håləꝁå^{h}	*ṣåraŧ*	*bito*^{w}	*wəniŝe'ŧ*	*lə'åḥi*^{y}*w*
went	the fellow wife of	his daughter	and marryPAR	to his brother

haššeni^{y}	...	*umeŧ*	(1:2)[7]
the second	...	and diedMASC	

'if the fellow-wife of his daughter went and married his other brother ... and then (that brother) died'

wəhål ꝁå^{h}	*habbaŧ*	*wəni*^{y}*ŝŝe't*	*lə'ɛƀɛđ*	*'o*^{w}	*ləꝁu*^{w}*ŧi*^{y}
and went	the daughter	and marryPAR	to slave	or	to gentile

wəyåləđå^{h}	*he*^{y}*mɛnnu*^{w}	*ƀen*	(7:5)
and bore	from him	son	

'and the daughter went and married a slave or a gentile and had a son from him'

wəhåləꝁå^{h}	*habbaŧ*	*wəni*^{y}*ŝŝeŧ*	*ləꝁohen*	*wəyål đå*^{h}	*he*^{y}*mɛnnu*^{w}	*ƀen* (7:6)
and went	the daughter	and marryPAR	to priest	and bore	from him	son

'and the daughter went and married a priest and had a son from him'

All are backgrounds to laws and may be read as though prefaced by, "In cases where it has happened that..." I can only explain the strange series of tenses (past, participle, past) as the result of lax style, perhaps attributable to the "personal notes" character of the text; apparently, the text was originally written as notes in personal notebooks to aid memory, with little attempt at a polished style (see, for example, Peretz (1967:24-28)) Clearly, each example is a story, with three consecutive events; such a narrative is normally rendered with past tense in MH. In the many cases cited by Kasovski

[6]'Shoe-removal' is a symbolic act performed when the man concerned refuses to perform levirate marriage.

[7]'MarryPAR' has different spellings in the text, as shown by the transliteration, but there is no question that the same word is intended.

(1967) of 'went' followed by another verb to convey a series of events, the great majority display the verb which follows 'went' conjugated in the past tense. The example at hand is therefore the exception to the rule.

Surely, the participle here is not doing anything that it did in BH, and so at least in terms of our research we cannot say that the development of the participle has not yet reached the stage that I claimed for it. These examples are indeed ones of reference by narrative, but they are odd examples, which, especially because of their negligible number, do not seem to indicate much about how the participle refers to time in MH in general. Also, since 'went and marryPAR' appears a few times in exactly the same form, there is the possibility that it is an idiomatic usage, in which case it does not affect my discussion at all.

We have, then, participles which refer to time, by and large, by being unbounded, or rather the time reference is inherent in their morphology. In a small percentage of the cases, the reference is given by an auxiliary verb, *håyå*^{h}.

3.2.3. What Time Does the Participle Refer to?

3.2.3.1. General Time Reference

It is not easy to determine what time the participle refers to because the "general time" which I discussed above is of a peculiar kind. It is used in 59.3% of its occurrences to state laws, and in another 13.2% of the cases in the formula 'such and such says', which introduces a legal opinion usually at variance with other opinions. For example:

In the statement of law:

hăre^{y} *'ellu*^{w} *ḥo*^{w}*ləṣo*^{w}*ŧ* (3:9)
here these-FEM perform shoe removal
'these (categories of women) perform shoe-removal'

In the introduction of a legal opinion:

rabbi^{y} *yəhu*^{w}*đå*^{h} *'o*^{w}*mer* *hannśu*^{w}*'o*^{w}*ŧ* *yiŧ'årəsu*^{w} ...
Rabbi Yehuda sayPAR the married ones will become betrothed ...

rabbi *yo*^{w}*se*^{y} *'o*^{w}*mer* *kɔl* *hannåši*^{y}*m* *yiŧ'år su*^{w} (4:10)
Rabbi Yosey sayPAR all the women will become betrothed

'Rabbi Yehuda says, the married ones (whose husbands died) are allowed to become betrothed (right away) ... (whereas) Rabbi Yosey says, all women are allowed to become betrothed'

In such cases it is hard to pinpoint a "present tense" or the moment of speech. 'Perform shoe removal' is true whenever an appropriate situation occurs; similarly, 'Rabbi Yehuda says' his opinion, so to speak, whenever one considers the legal question that he addressed. Of course, in both cases we have general time, but this is not a situation where a clear distinction is possible between the general time meaning and the present tense meaning. Rather, this general time is as close to the meaning of "present" as these contexts will allow.

It is relevant here to see the only case where the participle fulfills a clearly concurrent present tense function:

'åmar *låhɛm* *lo'* *ꝁi*^{y} *hălåꝁå*^{h} *'ăni*^{y} *'o*^{w}*mer* (8:3)
he said to them no indeed a law I sayPAR
'he told them, "No, it is a law that I am stating (and not just my opinion)"'

This is a very telling example of everyday style, not legalese, where the present tense is used most naturally. The reason that our text does not include more such examples is only that it does not include much narrative. Significantly, no form other than the participle is charged with conveying concurrent time, or present tense reference; that is, there is no other place in the text where such clear reference to concurrent time is found but where a form other than the participle is utilized. Present tense, then, is the exclusive domain of the participle.

The conclusion is that the participle is a means to convey general time, but not to the exclusion of the present tense. In fact, despite the scarcity of concurrent participles, and considering the limitations of the text, one can estimate with some certainty that the present tense function was very closely, most likely exclusively, associated with the participle. In the literature there is general agreement that the participle has become present tense in MH, at least generally speaking. See, for example, the Encyclopaedia Judaica (1971:vol. 16, 1600); Peretz (1967:38); Driver (1892:169); Segal (1909:24); Bendavid (1967:129) and Rabin (1960:30-31).

We continue now and reach the participles that have preceding-time reference. They include three cases that receive time reference by narrative. I mentioned above (section 3.2.2) that they seem to have been carelessly written, and in any event the use of the participle in them to refer to preceding time is very odd, especially as it is one event in a series and is flanked by past tense on both sides. I have little to add here other than to say that to draw any conclusions on the basis of these examples would be rash. The other three cases of preceding time reference are the case of 'they refrained (from) doing' discussed above in this section, and two cases of *håyå*^{h} + participle, discussed in section 3.3. below. In these cases the *håyå*^{h} and the verb 'refrained' serve as auxiliary verbs. They confer a preceding time reference on the participle; the participle itself has none.

Thus, the time reference associated with the participle is seen as one of a general/concurrent time in the main, and it is inherent in the form rather than assigned to it by external devices in the great majority of the cases.

3.2.3.2. Future and Past "Compete" with the Participle for General Time Reference?

Given that the present tense function is always performed by the participle, one still faces another interesting problem: the statement of law, which most of the participles in the text are used for, is also carried by the future form, and, to a lesser extent, by the past form, as shown in the time-reference table. The breakdown is as follows:

Participle: 60% of all time referenced verb forms used for law
Future: 34.2% of all time referenced verb forms used for law
Past: 5.8% of all time referenced verb forms used for law

3.2.3.2.1. Future for the Statement of Law

True, the future is used in many fewer cases than the participle, but as the table shows, 91% OF ALL FUTURE FORMS in the text are used for law. For example,

kohen	*gåđo*^{w}*l*	*lo'*	*yiśśå'*	*'almånå*^{h}	(6:4)
priest	big	not	will marry	widow	

'a high priest shall not marry a widow'

yiśrå'el	*šɛbbå'*	*'al*	*bat*	*kohen*	*to'ꝁal*	*biŧru*^{w}*må*^{h}
Israelite	that came	on	daughter of	priest	she will eat	in priest's due

'if an Israelite should have sexual intercourse with a priest's daughter, she still has the right (she has not lost the right) to eat of the "priest's due" (a kind of sacrifice)'

These seem to be cases where the BH usage has not disappeared, i.e. in BH, much law is given in the prefix verb form. However, I believe it is not justified to draw conclusions from this fact regarding the status of the participle or, for that matter, regarding the future form. Rather, conclusions must be drawn regarding forensic MH. In MH, law can be stated either as a regulation to be carried out in the future (such as the English *Violators will be towed away*), and in that case future tense is used; or the law can be stated as a rule which is always followed (such as *A person who kills goes to prison*), and then it is stated with the participle fulfilling the general time function discussed above. It is thus not true to say that the prefix form competes with the participle for the general time function; rather, some laws are simply stated for subsequent time, and then, quite naturally, the future form is used.

Against my opinion one could claim that future morphology can be used to convey general time or present meaning. Here are English examples:

> Q: *Where's John?*
> A: *Oh, he'll be in the library now.* (Usage limited to the verb *be*)[8]

(Future refers to concurrent time.)

> *Unscrupulous politicians will accept bribes.*

(Future has general-time meaning.)

However, notice that in both examples the future adds a special coloring to the meaning. In the first sentence, there is the suggestion that the answer is a guess; in the second, *will* actually means 'are likely to'. This is different from stating laws, even in English. Compare the above to *A person who uses a gun in the commission of a crime will go to jail.* This *will* doubtlessly refers to the future; it does NOT mean 'is likely to go to jail', or 'usually goes to jail'. I stand, therefore, by my original opinion, i.e. in our text, the future does not vie with the participle for the general time or present meanings.

3.2.3.2.2. Past for the Statement of Law

To conclude the examination of potential competitors to the participle in the statement of law I reach now the fourteen cases of past tense rendering law. Whereas I could not find a semantic or pragmatic reason for the choice between participle and future for that purpose, there is a clear semantic reason for the use of the past. It appears when the very performance of a given act automatically brings a certain consequence into effect. The past verbs used are *zåꝁå*^{h} 'won, received' (4:7), *qånå*^{h} 'acquired' (6:1), and twelve cases of *påsal* 'disqualified' (6:2, 8:5–four times, 10:3, 10:6–twice, 10:7–twice, 10:8–twice). Here is an example:

habbå'	*'al*	*yəƀimto*^{w}	...	*qånå*^{h}	(6:1)
the comePAR	on	his widowed sister-in-law	...	acquired	

'he who copulates with his widowed sister-in-law has (thereby) made her his wife'

This is not a ruling like, "He must now marry her," or "He will marry her." Neither the people involved nor the court must do anything else. The very act has automatically put the two in a state of wedlock. The use of the past stresses the fact that the consequence is already in effect; therefore the verb in the past tense actually refers to PRECEDING time, seeing that the law itself examines the situation AFTER the commission of the act. Hence we find again that the participle as a general time verb conveying law is unrivaled.

3.2.3.3. "Habitual/Iterative in Preceding" Time Reference

The habitual/iterative in preceding time reference is rendered twice with *håyå*^{h}. All of the cases of *håyå*^{h} are discussed immediately below. The other case of habitual in preceding time is an example discussed above (section 3.2.2), i.e.

---

[8]Robert Hetzron, personal communication.

nimnə‘u^{w}	*‘o*^{w}*ṡi*^{y}*n*	(1:3)
they refrained	doPAR-PL	
‘they refrained from doing’		

Here it seems that ‘refrained’ gives time reference to the participle. ‘Refrained’ cannot, of course, be regarded as an auxiliary verb, having its own semantic content as a separate verb. Therefore, this participle receives its time reference from a higher verb. This, then, is one example where the participle has not yet acquired inherent time reference.

Still, it is much more common in MH to use the infinitive rather than the participle in constructions like this, and in MnH the infinitive is always used to the exclusion of the participle in such cases. Segal (1909:49) records two more examples of a participle after ‘refrained’ and a number of examples where the occurrence of the participle is dependent on other verbs, e.g. *hiṫḥi*^{y}*l* ‘began’, just as it is here dependent on the occurrence of ‘refrained’. These then are governed usages of the participle. Segal also mentions that in these examples “we would normally expect the infinitive” (rather than the participle). The scarcity of such constructions and the fact that they show a grammaticized pattern of a governed participle leave intact the picture of time reference inherent in the form of the participle.

To conclude the discussion of the cases of time reference derived from the context, I might point out an interesting fact: whereas in BH the participle could simply receive, say, preceding-time reference such that it would be equivalent to a past tense verb, in MH, even if it does refer to preceding time, it gives its own coloring to the time reference in 50% of the cases, i.e. habitualness/iterativity. To that extent, the participle has its inherent time reference, which is rarely ignorable even when combined with another time reference from the context.

3.3. *håyå*^{h} with the Participle

We have seen how in LBH (Nehemiah) the *håyå*^{h} before a participle changes from a copula which is also a time indicator to an auxiliary. It begins fulfilling two functions for the participle: it carries the time reference and also indicates repeated action. In MH, *håyå*^{h} continues the trend begun in Nehemiah, i.e. it works as an auxiliary to provide time reference to the participles that it accompanies and it also adds to the meaning.

TABLE 10.
Functions of *håyå*^{h}

PROVIDES PRECEDING TIME REFERENCE	2
PROVIDES ITERATIVE OR CONTINUOUS MEANING (OVERLAPS ABOVE CATEGORY)	2
PROVIDES MODAL MEANING	2

Altogether there are four cases of *håyå*^{h} + participle in the text.
An example of the iterative function of *håyå*^{h} is:

kɔl	*haṭṭɔhɔ̆ro*^{w}*ṫ*	*wəhaṭṭu*^{w}*m’o*^{w}*ṫ*	*šɛhåyu*^{w}	*’ellu*^{w}	*məṭahari*^{y}*n*
all	the cleanness	and the uncleanness	that were	these	declare cleanPAR

wə’ellu^{w}	*məṭammə’i*^{y}*n*	...	(1:4)
and these	declare uncleanPAR ...		

'In all the disputed cases regarding cleanness and uncleanness, where one school would declare (the people concerned) clean and the other school would declare (them) unclean ... '

'Were' plus 'declare' are to be read as a repeated, preceding-time action, 'would declare', or 'used to declare'.

An example of the modal *håyå*^{h} is:

'im	*håyå*^{h}	*ḥo*^{w}*leṣ*	*ḥo*^{w}*leṣ*	*lappəsu*^{w}*lå*^{h}	(4:11)
if	he was	remove shoePAR	remove shoePAR	to the ineligible	

'if he would submit to shoe-removal, he receives shoe-removal from the woman ineligible to marry'

The *håyå*^{h}, and the other example (also in 4:11), which is almost identical in its use, provide subjunctive modality. The above example means, considering the context, "If the man concerned were willing to submit to shoe-removal, which signifies that he is not going to marry the woman performing the ceremony, then at least he should receive the shoe-removal from the woman whom he cannot marry because of objective reasons anyway." The conditionality is provided by 'if'; the modality is provided by the *håyå*^{h}.

Now to draw conclusions from the above facts. As I mentioned in the discussion of *håyå*^{h} in BH, the *håyå*^{h} + participle construction is one where the participle still exhibits the visible qualities of an intermediate form, the mold cast for a semi-noun, which at one time required a time reference indicator or a copula. However, a reanalysis has taken place. *håyå*^{h} + participle is not simply a verb with preceding time reference which can parallel a verb in the past tense; rather, it has its own interpretation which is verbal rather than nominal. The participle is drawing away from its intermediate form function towards becoming a verb, and accordingly, the *håyå*^{h} is reanalyzed AS AN AUXILIARY. Notice that even when the *håyå*^{h} provides time reference, it also provides iterativity, i.e. it is an auxiliary verb.

In the literature, observations about the *håyå*^{h} + participle construction in MH are made that are similar to mine but in a rather brief and general way. Thus Peretz (1967:38) calls the meaning associated with this construction "repeated action"; Segal (1909:50) talks about iterative action or action continuing along a period of time; Bendavid (1967:538) says much the same thing. The Encyclopaedia Judaica (1971:vol. 16, 1600) observes repeated or concurrent action, the latter standing for an action which occurs as background to another, shorter action. This last function of the construction is not attested in my text. Segal also says that the participle has no reference to time by itself and is therefore assigned the *håyå*^{h} to provide that reference, but it should be clear at this point that that is not the case. To mention just one point, the small percentage of participles with *håyå*^{h} leaves open the big question of how the other time referenced participles receive their time reference.

In conclusion, then, the *håyå*^{h} + participle continues in MH the trend begun in LBH, namely, it serves as a complex verb which includes an auxiliary and a main verb.

3.4. The Participle as an Intermediate Form

In this section I examine to what extent the participle still appears as a form clearly serving both a verbal and a nominal function. The parameters of investigation, represented as the categories in the table below, must first be explained. The first category is "verb + noun". By that label I refer to constructions such as

hakko^{w}*nes*	*'et*	*yəbimto*^{w}	(2:8)
the marryPAR	ACC	his sister-in-law	

'he who marries his (widowed) sister-in-law'

Here the participle has a clear sentence element, namely, a direct object, which points towards a verbal classification. But consider

uꝁnåsåh *hammǝǥåreš* *umeŧ* (3:7)
and married her the divorcePAR and died
'and the one who had divorced (his wife) married her (i.e. a second wife) and (then he) died'

Here the participle appears by itself and is totally interchangeable with any noun such as, say, 'the man'. Still, it is entirely possible to imagine a direct object following this participle, much as a direct object follows the participle in the first example above. Then the NP might read

hammǝǥåreš *'eŧ* *'išto*^{w}
the divorcePAR ACC his wife
'he who divorces his wife'

One way of viewing these participles is as agentive nouns, similar to *-er* nouns in English such as *writer, painter*, etc. This would explain the definite article *ha-* and the distribution of the participles in the last two of the above examples. However, this analysis does not explain the sentence elements, i.e. the direct object.

The other possible analysis is to view these participles as headless relatives, that is, as verbal rather than nominal in nature. Recall that *ha-*, or agreement in definiteness with the head, is a possible indicator of a relative clause which begins with a participle. We could posit an ellipted definite noun such as *hå'i*^{y}*š* 'the man' before each of the above participles. One supporting fact is that, when the "verb + noun" participle is definite, one never finds a relative clause following such participles. If these participles are simply nouns, why would they not take relative clauses? However, if the participles are relatives themselves, then the lack of relatives modifying them is not surprising. The problem with this analysis is demonstrated in the following example:

šo^{w}*mereŧ* *yåƀåm* *šenåᵽlu*^{w} *la*^{h} *nǝꝁasi*^{y}*m* (4:3)
watchPAR-FEM of levirate marriage who fell to her property
'a woman awaiting levirate marriage who has inherited property'

In 4:9 and 6:4 similar constructions appear. The participle here appears in a construct, i.e. a possessive construction, typically reserved for NOUNS. On the other hand, the semantics of the construction would present the 'levirate marriage' as a direct object, and the participle thus appears as having VERBAL force. Then again, it has no definite article and it is followed by a relative clause, which makes it impossible to view it as a headless relative.

In conclusion, then, these participles display a mixed collection of qualities, some verbal, some nominal; it is only if we allow for an "intermediate" category, namely, a category halfway between nominal and verbal, that we can explain all the facts.

The second category in the table is "verb + adjective", which includes cases like

habbå' *'al* *yǝƀimto*^{w} ... *'åᵽi*^{y}*lu*^{w} *hu*^{w}*'* *so*^{w}*ǥeg*
the copulatePAR on his sister-in-law ... even he errPAR

wǝhi^{y}*'* *mǝzi*^{y}*đå̊*^{h} (6:1)
and she act on purposePAR ...

'he who copulates with his (widowed) sister-in-law ... even if he act in error/be mistaken and she act on purpose/be purposive ... '

As the gloss indicates, the participles for 'err' and 'act on purpose' are intermediate forms, interpretable as adjectives or verbs.

And as for the last category, sometimes the participle can be taken only as a noun. For example,

kohen	*gådo^wl*	...	*lo'*	*yiššå'*	*'ɛt*	*habbo^wgerɛt*	(6:4)
priest	big	...	not	will marry	ACC	the maturePAR-FEM	

'a high priest ... will not marry a woman who has reached maturity'

Here the participle cannot be taken as verbal, i.e. 'a woman who is maturing'. It can only be taken as a nominal. Such cases I counted as examples of participles used exclusively as nouns.

TABLE 11.
The Participle as an Intermediate Form and as a Noun

AS AN INTERMEDIATE FORM	VERB + NOUN	30 (11.9% of total participles)
	VERB + ADJECTIVE	13 (5.2% of total participles)
AS A NOUN EXCLUSIVELY		2 (0.8% of total participles)

Compared to the percentages in BH the findings here do not show the tendency noted in other tables:

in EBH, 16.2% of all participles are intermediate forms;
in LBH, 6.1% of all participles are intermediate forms;
in MH, 17.1% of all participles are intermediate forms.

As for "exclusively nouns," they decrease: 6.2% in BH and 0.8% in MH.

So, while in BH the development is away from the intermediate form, i.e. the participle becomes either a noun or a verb, in BH there is extensive use of the intermediate form. I can offer only a partial explanation of why in this particular case one does not find the same direction of development as in the categories examined before. Certainly, the facts of BH show that there is no inherent quality of the intermediate form that makes it more resistant to change. Perhaps, however, an explanation can be based on the peculiar stylistic demands that the users of MH were under, namely, the need for brevity. The headless relative (I shall call it that although, of course, there are problems in the labeling of this construction) is a useful construction for one who wishes to take quick, brief notes to facilitate retention of spoken material. Bear in mind that such notes are the earliest written form of the Mishnah. This is so simply because it saves writing the head of the relative, which will often be redundant in any case. In such cases the discussion refers to a person solely by the characterization contained in the relative, and so the head would have been 'the man who' or 'he who'. Such a demand for brevity does not obtain in BH, of course. Furthermore, because of the subject matter, i.e. laws, these headless relatives are most likely to include participles. Perhaps this is why the use of the intermediate form in MH manifests a certain increase as compared to BH.

3.5. Relative Clauses

In the following table, the term "headless relative" refers to participles with the definite article as described at the beginning of section 3.4. All counted cases have the definitizer serving as a relativizer and a direct object or a complement which could be sentence elements. The more questionable cases, as described in the section on the intermediate form (section 3.4) were not counted. Still, since even those cases which can more clearly be identified as headless relatives have a semi-nominal character, their number is kept separate in the table from the number of relatives with heads. In the text, there are no relative clauses with a verb in the future. Past relatives are the only relatives other than participle relatives.

The meaning of "otherwise conditioned" and "not otherwise conditioned" in the table is the same as in the discussion of relatives in BH, namely, if the relativizer appears separated from the participle, then it cannot be the definitizer *ha-*, but must be *šɛ* (a discussion of *šɛ-* vs. *'ăšɛr* follows). This is the "otherwise conditioned' occurrence of *šɛ-*. However, if the relativizer appears immediately before the participle, then it can be either *ha-* or *šɛ-*; if *šɛ-* appears, it appears because the participle is regarded as a verb, and *šɛ-* is the relativizer used with verbs. This is the occurrence of *šɛ-* that is conditioned by the verbal nature of the participle, "not otherwise conditioned."

TABLE 12
Relative Clauses

			WITH HEAD	HEADLESS	TOTAL
ALL RELATIVES			62	21	83
RELATIVES WITH PAR		TOTAL	18 (29% of all rel's with head)	21 (100% of all headless rel's)	39
RELATIVES WITH PAR		SUBJECT REL'S	16 (88.8% of PAR rel's with head)	21 (100% of headless PAR rel's)	37 (94.9% of all PAR rel's)
RELATIVES WITH PAR		NON-SUBJ. REL'S	2 (11.1% of PAR rel's with head)	0	2 (5.1% of all PAR rel's)
RELATIVES WITH TENSE OTHER THAN PAR (ALL ARE PAST)		TOTAL	44 (71% of all rel's with head)	0	44
RELATIVES WITH TENSE OTHER THAN PAR (ALL ARE PAST)		SUBJECT REL'S	31 (70.5% of non-PAR rel's with head)	0	31 (70.5% of non-PAR rel's)
RELATIVES WITH TENSE OTHER THAN PAR (ALL ARE PAST)		NON-SUBJ. REL'S	13 (29.5% of non-PAR rel's with head)	0	13 (29.5% of non-PAR rel's)
RELATIVIZER	PAR RELATIVES	*ha-*	2 (11.1% of PAR rel's with head)	21 (100% of headless PAR rel's)	23 (59% of PAR rel's)
RELATIVIZER	PAR RELATIVES	*šɛ-* OTHERWISE CONDITIONED	4 (22.2% of PAR rel's with head)	0	4 (10.3% of PAR rel's)
RELATIVIZER	PAR RELATIVES	*šɛ-*, NOT OTHERWISE CONDITIONED	12 (66.6% of PAR rel's with head)	0	12 (30.8% of PAR rel's)
RELATIVIZER	TENSED REL'S (NON-PAR)	*ha-*	0	0	0
RELATIVIZER	TENSED REL'S (NON-PAR)	*šɛ-*	44 (100% of non-PAR rel's with head)	0	44 (100% of non-PAR rel's)

A striking fact is that most relatives in the text are subject relatives. This fact must be attributed to the style of the genre, which is characterized by repeated formulaic sentences and phrases. Still, the following conclusions can be drawn: in BH 78% of the participle relatives were subject relatives, whereas (at least in the ten chapters of I Kings) 75.2% of the TENSED relatives were NON-subject relatives. I concluded there that the participle was regarded as adjective-like. In MH the ratio is much more equal (in relatives with heads): 88.8% of the participle relatives and 70.5% of the past relatives are subject relatives. Hence, the direction of development predicted in the discussion of BH materializes. As the participle loses its intermediate form character (in this case, it becomes more verb-like) participle relatives become similar to relatives with other tenses. This characterization does not apply to headless relatives. They retain the original character of the participle, as I concluded in section 3.4, and the figures prove it: all headless relatives are subject relatives and use the participle.

The relativizer continues the development begun in BH. As I explained above (section 2.5.1), *šɛ-* was the relativizer used in the more colloquial dialect destined to become MH, while *'ăšer* was its more formal BH counterpart. Recall also that in LBH the use of *šɛ-* increases. In MH the process is completed, and *šɛ-* is used to the exclusion of *'ăšer*.

All non-subject relatives and all past tense relatives display *šɛ-*, but the participle relatives still have *ha-*, the definite article, in 59% of the cases. In 10% of the cases *šɛ-* is utilized with the participle for a reason that makes the use of *ha-* impossible, such as non-contiguity of the participle and the head, where definiteness agreement cannot be present (as explained in section 2.5.1). However, in 30.8% of the cases we find *šɛ-* where *ha-* could very well appear. If we exclude headless relatives from consideration, then the cases of "not otherwise conditioned" *šɛ-* constitute 66.6% of the total participle relatives. This is compared with 6.5% of "not otherwise conditioned" *šɛ-* in BH. In greater detail:

"not otherwise conditioned" *šɛ-* in EBH–2.6% of participle relatives
"not otherwise conditioned" *šɛ-* in LBH–10.6% of participle relatives
"not otherwise conditioned" *šɛ-* in MH –30.8% of participle relatives
or 66.6% of participle relatives

The direction of development is obvious. As the participle gradually becomes verbal, the verbal relativizer begins to accompany it more and more. This being the case, one may very well question the "otherwise conditioned" *šɛ-* cases. Did they receive *šɛ-* only because *ha-* would not be possible, or, seeing that so many participles receive *šɛ-* where *ha-* IS possible, perhaps these "otherwise conditioned" cases too would have received *šɛ*, even if *ha-* were possible? The fact that this possibility can be entertained provides further demonstration of the change of the nature of the participle and the consequent change in the relativizer that the participle takes.

3.6. Word Order—How the Participle Pushed towards SVO

For the following table, I counted sentences that did not display a reason for the word order to be marked. Thus I excluded questions sentences with no overt subject, sentences with fronting for emphasis or contrast, and sentences with sentence-initial adverbs, which push the subject to post-verbal position.

TABLE 13.
Unmarked Word Order in Independent Clauses

ORDER	PAST	FUTURE	PARTICIPLE
SVO	6	35	29
VSO	42	7	0

This table shows that the participle appears exclusively in SVO, which is expected in light of the discussion of word order in BH (section 2.6). This order is noticed by Segal (1909:46), Bendavid (1967:808), and others. However, the table also shows a startling association between SVO and future tense and between VSO and past tense. To understand these figures, recall that 92.1% of all future tense verbs are used to state law (see the discussion in section 3.2.3.2). This use of a verb form is not one to which verbs are put in everyday spoken language and is therefore not very instructive for determining basic, unmarked word order. The past, in which, among other things, the few cases of simple narrative are related, is a much better candidate for that purpose. We can therefore conclude that there is reason to take VSO, the unmarked word order of BH, as the unmarked order of MH as well.

However, the more interesting point is the following: since the participle, as I showed above, is the most natural medium to convey law, it seems that the SVO order always associated with the participle has become identified as the order in which law is conveyed and has been extended to ANY tense when that tense is used to state law. I discussed, in the chapter on BH, how SVO order spreads from semi-nominal constructions (those with participles) to regular sentences once the participle is reanalyzed as a regular verb. Here now is another avenue in which SVO order spreads from the participle to other verbs. Because the participle is used for the statement of law, SVO in general becomes associated with the statement of law and spreads to any tense used for that purpose.

To buttress this conclusion, consider the singular fact that of the fourteen cases where PAST tense is used to state law, seven have a clear SVO order, and the other seven have no overt subject at all. There is not one case where even the past tense, when used for law, displays its natural VSO order. Rather, it appears in SVO, the word order copied from participle sentences because it became associated with the statement of law.

3.7. Negation

We saw that in BH the participle is negated by the noun negator *'e^{y}n*, 'there is not' exclusively. The situation in MH is as follows:

'e^{y}n—15 cases, 29.4% of total participle negation
lo' —36 cases, 70.6% of total participle negation

The verb negator is *lo'* 'no'. In this regard too, then, the participle is becoming more and more verb-like. Segal (1909:43-46) admits that *lo'* is used to negate participles in MH but adds that *lo'* is constrained in the following manner: it appears only when there is special emphasis to the negation, or when the negated participle appears immediately after a positive verb, or when two negative participles appear in a sequence. I found that his restriction that there be an adjacent participle, negative or positive, can in fact be held, although I am convinced that it would take exegetic acrobatics to prove special emphasis in every other *lo'* negative. The amazing part is Segal's conviction that, because of the constraints on the co-occurrence of *lo'* with participles, this co-occurrence cannot be taken as an indication that the participle has shifted towards becoming a regular verb in MH. This he asserts despite his admission that the participle is assuming the role of the present tense in MH (1909: 24). It seems that, Segal's objection notwithstanding, the negation of the participle does point to the verbalization that it undergoes.

3.8. Circumstantial Adverbials

In my text there is no construction similar to the circumstantial adverbial of BH. However, Segal (1909:50) talks about what he calls a "circumstantial clause" and cites the following example (not taken from the text I surveyed):

šå'altiʸ	*'ɛṯ*	*rabbån*	*gamliʸ'el*	*'oʷmeḏ*	*bəša'ar*	*hammizråḥ* ...
I asked	ACC	Teacher	Gamliel	standPAR	in the gate of	the east ...

'I asked the scholar Gamliel, when he was standing at the eastern gate ... '

(Order Zraim, Tractate Orla, 2:12)

This use of the participle fits the criteria established in the discussion of BH for the circumstantial adverbial. Peretz too mentions (1967:40) the existence of this construction but adds that in MH an innovation appears in some circumstantial clauses: they are subordinated by *kəšɛ-*, 'when'.

All in all, the circumstantial adverbial is still present in MH, but the lack of any such example in my text indicates that at least the frequency of occurrence of this usage of the participle is noticeably lower in MH than in BH. Also, in some cases a subordinator (*kəšɛ-*) is present, as is the case always with past and future verbs. The tendency then is for the participle to lose its special character which allowed it to signify subordination and become a regular verb which requires a subordinator lest it be understood as another action in a series rather than a circumstantial adverbial.

To conclude the discussion of MH I would like to point out that all the criteria that I used to measure BH by except one (the "intermediate form") show at least a definite progress towards reanalysis of the participle in MH as a verb. Still, the process is not complete, and some "intermediate" qualities remain associated with the participle. The end point of the process can be observed in MnH, to which the next chapter is devoted.

4. MODERN HEBREW

4.1. Introduction

4.1.1. The Nature of Modern Hebrew

There still exists in Israel an ideological principle which was used in providing the immense number of innovations required by Hebrew as a revived language, namely, that one looks to the language of the Sources (Bible, Mishnah, and other works) as a model on which to fashion the required constructions and vocabulary items. The Bible, therefore, is always "correct" Hebrew, and in writing one may use almost any Biblical construction, marking one's style as more or less formal or lofty, depending in part on the rareness of the construction. Written MnH is therefore a very elusive language to work with. Changes and developments are really best attested in the Hebrew used among friends in casual conversation, among children outside the classroom, and generally among people when they are not concerned with the linguistic "correctness" of what they say, and therefore use the least assuming and most natural style.

This is a distinction of the utmost importance. It is not a simple matter such as excluding from the data the language of anybody with more than eight years of school. Rather, this is often a matter of weighing and comparing usages for the purpose of deciding which is a more formal usage, typical of learned style, and which is a more natural comfortable usage, representative of the direction in which the language is developing.

The Hebrew that emerges as relevant to us from such an examination is what I shall refer to as MnH. There is, of course, no direct continuity between MH and MnH. The people who revived the language, being for the most part speakers of European languages with tripartite verb systems, most likely preferred the MH verb system to the EBH one because of their native languages. The facts about MnH to be discussed below are doubtlessly affected by this influence of European languages.

4.1.2. The Starting Point

As I showed above, the BH participle was, generally speaking, a form whose classificatory range extended from the nominal (noun and adjective-like) on the one hand to the almost verbal (verb-like, but without tense for time reference) on the other. Then two forces started to exert pressure towards change. The first force was a vacuum created by the shift in Hebrew from a dual to a tripartite tense system in the verb. There were natural candidates for the function of the past and the future, namely, the suffixed and prefixed forms respectively. The suffixed form had been used mostly for preceding time, the prefixed form for subsequent time, and in the tripartite system they generally continued fulfilling their respective functions. But another form became necessary now, one which would refer to concurrent time. This is the vacuum that was created in the verb system. The participle, which, when not affected by context time-reference, provided general time, was closest to what was required. It indicated that the entity (action or event) related was GENERALLY true, and so it was obviously true "right now", at the time of speech. Thus the participle moved in to fill the vacuum by taking on the function of the present tense.

The second force pressing towards a change is internal to the participle itself. As I mentioned above, time reference by inference and unbounded time reference increase in LBH. Simultaneously, the percentage of inferred-time participles which refer to concurrent time increases too. At some point, the speakers become conditioned to seeing participles as referring, as a matter of course, to concurrent or general time, with no need for the speaker or hearer to consider the context of every single participle in order to assign time reference to it. At that point the participle has changed into a tensed verb, and it exerts pressure to be given a recognized status in the verb system.

In MH we therefore see a tripartite system with the participle functioning as the present tense. In addition, a considerable number of participles refer to general time; they do so not by some external time indicator, but by the time reference inherent in them. Still, the participle in MH has not lost all of its previous characteristics. It still serves as an intermediate form, and in that capacity it has no inherent time reference on the one hand, and on the other hand it is not exclusively nominal.

In MnH, as we shall now see, the participle completes its development. In the following sections, I shall investigate each of the parameters used for BH and MH with respect to MnH, as well as some additional points.

4.2. Time Reference

In MnH, time reference for the participle is indicated exactly as it is indicated for other verbs, by tense. Some usages may remind one of the Biblical time reference by context, but in fact they are quite different. Consider the following:

(1) *bati* *laxeder* *veraiti* *et* *moše* *kotev* *mixtav*
I came to the room and I saw ACC Moshe writePAR letter
'I entered the room and saw Moshe writing a letter'

(2) *bati* *laxeder* *veraiti* *šemoše* *kotev* *mixtav*
I came to the room and I saw that Moshe writePAR letter
'I entered the room and saw that Moshe was writing a letter'

(3) *bati* *laxeder* *veraiti* *šemoše* *katav* *mixtav*
I came to the room and saw that Moshe wrote letter
'I entered the room and saw that Moshe had written a letter'

It might seem as though in sentences (1) and (2) the lower participle receives its time reference (preceding time) from the higher verb The writing of the letter obviously took place at the same time as the entrance into the room The fact, however, is different. The sequence-of-tenses rule which exists in English does not exist in Hebrew. Notice that the tenses in sentence (2) are not those found in its English translation; in the latter, past tense is clearly marked in the lower sentence too, while in Hebrew the present tense is used (as rendered by the participle). Following verbs of cognition like *raa* 'saw', *šama* 'heard', *gila* 'discovered', etc., and also following verbs of indirect speech like *amar* 'said', *taan* 'claimed', etc. (and even verbs not related to cognition or speech, as we shall see below), the tense used is exactly that which would be used if the sentence were a direct quote. For example:

(4) *moše amar, "ani oxel naknik."*
Moshe said, "I eatPAR sausage."
'Moshe said, "I am eating sausage."'

(5) *moše amar šeu oxel naknik*
Moshe said that he eatPAR sausage
'Moshe said that he was eating sausage'

In both sentences the verb 'eat' has the same tense, although one sentence has a direct quotation while the other has reported speech. Notice also that if you substitute past for the present in the lower verb in (2), thus creating (3), you get a past PERFECT meaning in the lower sentence.

Hence, in sentences (1) and (2) the participle is a present tense verb, not a tenseless intermediate form. And indeed, in sentences with verbs other than cognition or quotation verbs, a participle in a conjunct as in the Biblical circumstantial adverbial will simply not do. This is illustrated in sentences (6) and (7) below. This shows that the verb in the quoted clause is governed by the verb introducing that clause.

(6) **kšebati laxeder, moše kotev mixtav*
when I came to the room, Moshe writePAR letter
'when I entered the room, Moshe is writing a letter'

(7) **bati laxeder* { *uveoto zman* / *veaz* / *ve-* / *kše-* } *moše kotev mixtav*
I came to the room { and at the same time / and then / and / when } Moshe writePAR letter
'I entered the room { and at the same time / and then / and / when } Moshe is writing a letter'

These WOULD be acceptable if the tense in the second clause in each were changed to the past, i.e. *katav* 'wrote'.

Similarly, consider:

(8a) *bi^y 'ăđoni^y ... 'ăni^y hå'išå^h hanniṣeƀeŧ 'imꝁå^h båze^h* (I S.1.26)
in me my lord ... I the woman the standPAR with you in this
'Please, sir ... I am the woman who stood with you here'

(8b) *bevakaša adoni ... ani haiša šenicevet itxa ...*
in request, my lord ... I the woman that standPAR with you ...
Please, Sir ... I am the woman who is standing with you ... '

(Sentence (8b) is grammatical; however, it is not an acceptable paraphrase of (8a).)

(8c) *bevakaša adoni ... ani haiša šenicva itxa ...*
in request, my lord ... I the woman that stood with you ...
'Please, Sir ... I am the woman that stood with you ... '

Sentence (8a), when rendered in MnH as (8b) (the issue of *šɛ-* is discussed below), will not be an acceptable paraphrase; the participle unavoidably refers to concurrent time. The time reference in the relative MUST be shown by tense, as in (8c). Furthermore, adding the word *etmol* 'yesterday' will also not save (8b), whereas Biblical participles accept time reference from adverbs very readily. Thus, participles, if used as verbs, must be tensed. Otherwise, they are used as nouns.

The general time reference can be indicated in MnH by an adverb, such as *kol hazman* 'all the time'. The participle itself did retain general reference, but definitely as a feature in its own right, mutually exclusive of other time reference and not because the participle is unbounded. For example:

(9) *ex ata yaxol ledaber kaxa kšemoše makšiv?*
how you can to talk so when Moshe listenPAR?
'how can you talk like that when Moshe is listening?'

This sentence may be a comment on an event that occurred in preceding time or on one that is occurring in concurrent time. In the latter case there is no problem; the participle is fulfilling its most natural function as a present tense, concurrent time referenced verb. In the former case, however, it could be claimed that we have here a participle which refers to preceding time by inference, exactly like a BH participle. However the sentence itself does not have preceding time reference. Rather, the speaker has generalized from the past event and treats it as indicating a QUALITY of the addressee, the quality being "being able to talk like that when Moshe is listening". This quality is always there, and so the time reference of the sentence above is to general time.

Suppose we try to force preceding time interpretation on the participle. The following sentence is acceptable and seems to disprove my point:

(10) *ex yaxolta ledaber kaxa kšemoše makšiv?*
how you could to talk so when Moshe listenPAR?
'how could you talk like that when Moshe is listening?'

Here the first verb might seem to limit the interpretation of the participle (the second verb) to preceding time. But compare the above sentence to the unacceptable one below and the acceptable version following it:

(11) **lama dibarta kaxa kšemoše makšiv?*
why you talked so when Moshe listenPAR?
'why did you talk like that when Moshe is listening?'

(12) *lama dibarta kaxa kšemoše hikšiv?*
why you talked so when Moshe listened?
'why did you talk like that when Moshe was listening?'

Clearly (11) is bad because the two verbs force clashing time references on it. The participle is now a tensed verb in its own right and will not accept time reference from a fellow verb. When both verbs do agree in their time reference, as in (12), the sentence is acceptable.

Why, then, is (10) acceptable? This is because the unmatching time references are not in the same proposition and do not clash. The sentence can be paraphrased, "How could you (preceding time) have the quality of [talking like that (general time) when (or whenever) Moshe is listening (general time)]?" In simple syntactic terms, the lower sentence in (10) has no indication of preceding time (past tense) to clash with the general time indicated by the participle.

If general time is indeed an independent time reference feature, which clashes with non-general time reference, would it clash with a concurrent (present) time reference? Suppose we try to introduce a concurrent time verb before the general-time participle (we do this, of course, with a participle):

(13) *lama ata medaber kaxa kšemoše makšiv?*
why you talkPAR so when Moshe listenPAR?
'why do you talk like that when Moshe is listening?'

I think there is no way of avoiding reading the first verb as general too. It is certainly different from an admonition to a disruptive student in a classroom:

(14) *lama ata medaber?*
why you talkPAR?
'why are you talking?'

While (14) clearly carries concurrent time reference, (13) does not. It is general in both its verbs.

In conclusion, the MnH participle may have general time as its time reference, but unlike its BH ancestor (perhaps with the exception of the Nehemiah case), the MnH general time is a time reference mutually exclusive of other time references; also, it is internal to the verb, i.e. it is not taken on from the environment or arrived at because the participle is unbounded, and it has its own co-occurrence restrictions which, when violated, cause sentences to be unacceptable. One last remark with regard to Table 1: the continuous is not morphologically shown in MnH. It may be indicated adverbially, as with *kol oto zman*, 'all that time'. There seems to be no significant difference here between BH, MH, and MnH.

4.3. The Participle as a Non-Verb

As is clear from the discussion so far, a MnH participle will always be clearly classified as a nominal (noun or adjective) or as a verb. As a noun and as an adjective it may take the definite article; as a noun it may appear in a construct (a possessive construction); as a verb it will take various adverbs; and of course it will always function clearly as a nominal or as a verb in a sentence. In fact, I have reached the conclusion elsewhere (Gordon 1978) that in the lexicon of a synchronic grammar of MnH there is no place for a category such as the "intermediate form". In its nominal function the participle belongs in one category, and in its verbal function it belongs in another. Naturally, this state of affairs leads to ambiguity at times: *moše šomer* 'Moshe guardPAR', which presumably had one meaning originally—not quite verbal nor quite nominal—today must be classified and is clearly labeled in the mind of the speaker as either nominal or verbal, 'Moshe is a guard' or 'Moshe is guarding', respectively. The sentence would be disambiguated by the addition of the pronoun-copula *hu*, 'he/is' (indicating nominal use of the participle) or by an adverb like *hetev*, 'well' (indicating verbal use).

I should also mention that the participle is an automatically productive form only as a present tense. As a noun, it can be called semi-productive. By these terms I mean that any new verb coined in the language will automatically and without exception receive the participle morphology for its present tense, but a related nominal may be in any one of a number of nominal patterns, not necessarily that of the participle.

4.4. Circumstantial Adverbials

A BH conjunction where one of the members is a circumstantial adverbial with a participle will be regarded in MnH as a simple conjunction relating a sequence of events. Therefore the adverbial must be marked with *bizman še-* 'at the time that', *kše-* 'when', etc. Furthermore, the time reference of the adverbial must agree with that of the main clause. For example, the BH sentence (15) will be rendered as (16) in MnH:

(15)	*hemmå*^{h}	*'oli*^{y}*m*	*bəma'ăle*^{h}	*hå'i*^{y}*r*	*wəhemmå*^{h}	*måṣə'u*^{w}	*nə'åro*^{w}*ṯ*
	they	go upPAR	in the ascent of	the city	and they	found	girls ...

'as they went up on the way to the city they found girls ... ' (I S.9.11)

(16)	*kšeem*	*alu*	*baaliya*	*lair*	*hem*	*macu*	*nearot ...*
	when they	went up	in the uphill way	to the city	they	found	girls ...

'when they went up on the way to the city they met girls ... '

There is a colloquial stylistic device, used to increase the sense of realism in a narrative, which may be confusing here. This is the rendition of a preceding-time narrative in the present tense. For example (assume sentence is in a narrative which takes place in preceding time),

(17)	*kmo*	*šeani*	*ole*	*bamadregot*	*ani roe*	*et*	*moše ...*
	as	that I	go upPAR	in the stairs	I seePAR	ACC	Moshe ...

'as I climb the stairs I see Moshe ... '

Now this use of the present tense may be alternated with use of the past tense:

(18)	*kmo*	*šeani*	*ole*	*bamadregot*	*raiti*	*et*	*moše ...*
	as	that I	go upPAR	in the stairs	I saw	ACC	Moshe ...

'as I climbed the stairs I saw Moshe ... '

In this last usage, the adverbial may seem similar to the Biblical circumstantial adverbial; however, without the subordinating *kmo še-* 'as that', the sentence is definitely unacceptable:

(19)	**ani*	*ole*	*bamadregot*	*(ve)raiti*	*et*	*moše ...*
	I	go upPAR	in the stairs	(and) I saw	ACC	Moshe ...

'I climb the stairs (and) I saw Moshe ... '

Hence, it is not the presence of the participle which indicates the special status of the adverbial, as it does in BH; rather, it is the adverb 'as'. As for time reference, I tend to regard the present tense in (18) as a case of the realistic style device mentioned above. In this usage, the participle is not a non-time-referenced verb, but rather a verb referring to concurrent time. The reader or listener is informed that preceding time is intended by some other means, such as time adverbs ('yesterday'); but this preceding time reference IS NOT TRANSFERRED ONTO THE PARTICIPLE, which has its own time (concurrent). This, of course, is what makes this literary style effective in creating a greater sense of realism. The Biblical participle, which does assume preceding time reference in such sentences, has no such realistic effect at all. To conclude, with the emergence of the participle as a regular tensed verb, the syntactic phenomenon of the coordinated circumstantial adverbial disappears.

4.5. Relative Clauses with Participles

MnH relative clauses begin with *še-* 'that' exclusively. School grammars still teach that relatives with participles are to take agreement in definiteness as the relativizer, and in educated writing this practice prevails; but otherwise MnH has all but rejected this relativizer in favor of *še-*. In other words, participles, being regular verbs in MnH, take the same relativizer that other verbs take. Headless relatives, of the type widely utilized in MH, are most awkward in spoken MnH. Thus, a typical MH headless relative like

hammeƀi^{y}*’*	*geṭ*	*mimədi*^{y}*naŧ*	*hayyåm*	(2:9)
the bringPAR	divorce	from the country of	the sea	

‘he who brings a bill of divorce from a country across the sea’

would be rendered in MnH as

mi	*šemevi*	*get*	*mimdina*	*meever*	*layam*
who(ever)	that bringPAR	divorce	from a country	from over	to the sea

‘one who brings a bill of divorce from a country across the sea’

Since headless relatives are non-existent for past and future verbs, it is not surprising that they should be very awkward for the present tense as well.

4.6. Subject Position and the Shift to SVO

While unmarked word order in BH is VSO, in MnH it is SVO. The change is already evident in MH. The understanding we gained above of the development of the participle offers us an insight into the mechanics of word order change in general and the Hebrew word order change in particular. It indicates that the change from VSO to SVO in Hebrew was not a matter of, say, the verb suddenly moving to second position. No dramatic turning point is involved in the process. Rather, word order changed because of two processes, both of which involved reanalysis. Although unmarked word order in BH was VSO, sentences with participles were always subject-first in Hebrew. In BH, this word order did not constitute an exception to the rule, since the participle could not be considered a verb. In effect, then, an EBH participial sentence was very much like a nominal sentence, both consisting of a subject followed by a predicate nominal. Then the first process relevant to our discussion unfolded. The dual tense/aspect system changed to a tripartite tense system. As I remarked above, no dramatic change is involved, but a slow reanalysis. As a result of the change to a tripartite system, the participle is reanalyzed as a tensed verb. This is the second process leading towards the word order change. Once the participle became a verb, a major construction in the language, the participial sentence, was seen in a new light. Here was an SVO sentence. Thus a new situation arose, where the language was suddenly found to have a considerable stock of SVO sentences, both preserved in writing and spoken in everyday discourse. That stock, of course, was the stock of the sentences with participle predicates.

The next step was for this word order to spread into sentences with other verbs. A partial insight into this spreading process is provided in the chapter on MH. I showed there that evidently the statement of law became associated with the participle and hence with SVO order and that consequently when laws are stated in the future and in the past they too display SVO order. We thus see a chain reaction leading to the word order change, in which the development of the participle plays a key role.

Givón (1977:esp. 240), in a thorough study (concerned with BH exclusively), investigates the question from a different viewpoint and proposes different reasons for the word order change, but my view complements his to create a coherent picture. Givón sees topic shift, i.e. the introduction into the narrative of a different topic than the one previously used, as the reason for SV order in EBH. For topic shift, he says, the participle and the perfect were used, whereas the imperfect was used for relating the events of the narrative in chronological order. In LBH, Givón continues, the perfect and the participle were charged with the function of relating the narrative. Thus SV order, used with the perfect and the participle, became the prevalent word order.

This paper accepts the above and studies the participle using parameters of investigation different from Givón's. My conclusions complement Givón's in that I too see the participle as responsible in part for the shift to SVO order, albeit for reasons different from Givón's.

4.7. The Function of *haya*

In MnH, *haya* before a participle continues its function as an auxiliary if the participle is a verb and as a copula if the participle is a noun (*haya* is the MnH pronunciation and is the same verb rendered as $h\mathring{a}y\mathring{a}^{h}$ for BH and MH). These two uses of *haya* are a function of the polarization that occurred in the participle, namely, the change in its status from an intermediate form to either a noun or a verb in any given case.

The verb *haya* before a verbal participle is the only case of an auxiliary in MnH. It shows the time reference of the complex verb and in addition imparts any one of several meanings. It can indicate repeated action:

(20)	*bakayic*	*šeavar*	*hayiti*	*holex*	*layam*	*kol*	*šabat*
	in the summer	the past	I was	goPAR	to the sea	every	Saturday

'last summer I would go to the beach every Saturday'

It is also used in conditionals:

(21)	*im*	*hayita*	*mazmin*	*oti*	*hayiti*	*ba*
	if	you were	invitePAR	me	I was	comePAR

'had you invited me I would have come'

From conditionals, *haya* has expanded into polite requests:

(22)	*hayit*	*roca*	*lalexet*	*lataaruxa?*
	you were	wantPAR	to go	to the exhibition?

'would you like to go to the exhibition?'

Here the speaker is being polite by not demanding; he is giving the addressee an opportunity to refuse by recognizing that there may be many stumbling blocks on the way to granting his request. This is the reason for the conditional construction; it is as though the condition has been ellipted, and, if present, would have been, "If all obstacles could be overcome, would you ... ?"

A third use of *haya* is limited to some dialects. This is *haya* as the habitual or continuous auxiliary:

(23)	*kšebati*	*elav,*	*hu*	*haya*	*kore*	*sefer*
	when I came	to him	he	was	readPAR	book

'when I came to him, he was reading a book'

It is remarkable that in a language which used no auxiliaries, *haya* before a participle took on the function of an auxiliary so naturally, and it operates harmoniously with other verb forms which cannot take auxiliaries and must show distinctions like iterativity or habitualness in other ways. As I proposed in the section on *haya* in BH (section 2.7), the reluctance to change the APPEARANCE of constructions, e.g. to stop using *haya* before participles, is obviously greater than the resistance to reanalysis of the MEANING of those constructions.

4.8. Conclusion

The participle first appears, in BH, as an "intermediate" form, having some nominal and some verbal qualities. In LBH, a change in the participle is already noticeable; its time reference is received more and more in a way that would eventually become tense; its "intermediate" function decreases, so that greater differentiation is introduced between its nominal and its verbal functions; and various constructions, such as the circumstantial adverbial and the relative clause, when they include a participle, show a tendency to be marked differently as the nature of the participle changes. In MH the participle is markedly different from what it was in BH; its verbal qualities are made more definite, but it still has "intermediate" form qualities. In MnH, in every given case, the participle is either clearly verbal or clearly nominal. The "intermediate" function has disappeared altogether. The process of the polarization of the participle is completed.

APPENDIX: BERMAN'S STUDY

1. The Difference in Approach

The discussion in the last chapter found the MnH participle to have concluded the gradual change from an "intermediate" form to either a verb or a noun in every given case. However, Berman (1978: ch. 5), in a very detailed and comprehensive study, concludes that the verbal use of the participle still displays a number of qualities that distinguish it from past and future verbs. As should be clear at this point, I accept this conclusion as regards morphology and co-occurrence of the participle, but I see these qualities as idiosyncrasies of a VERB, not as indicative of an "intermediate" nature of the participle.

One major reason for the difference in our conclusions is that my objectives are different from Berman's. Her description of MnH is concerned with all levels of the language, such as literary usage, newspaper style, formal spoken language, and everyday colloquial speech. The reader will recall that my paper examines spoken, informal Hebrew exclusively, for the reason that this level of usage is the most instructive in tracing historical development.

Berman classifies a number of the characteristics which distinguish the participle from other verbs as typical of written or formal language, and not of everyday colloquial speech. I shall therefore not discuss these characteristics here. I do list below the other characteristics which she presents as peculiar to the participle, and I explain why they do not change my view of the participle as expressed in this paper.

2. Headless Relatives

Berman describes headless relatives of the form

(1) *harocim* *lalexet* *yerašmu* *kan*
the wantPAR to go will register here
'those wishing to go are to register here'

No verb form other than the participle can appear in headless relatives, and it could be claimed that the participle is functioning almost like a noun here, especially with the definite article *ha-* serving as the relativizer. However, I point out the fact that such headless relatives are rather formal, as the informal version of sentence (1) would be

(2) *mi* *šeroce* *lalexet* *yerašem* *kan*
who that want to go will register here
'whoever wishes to go is to register here'

In other words, the informal sentence has a relative with a head and with the normal relativizer, *še-*. This is the version most instructive about the end point in the historical development.

3. The Construct

Berman notes the fact that the participle can appear as the first member, or the "possessed" in a construct (the possessive construction). For example:

(3) *nearim* *xovšey* *kipot*
boys wearPAR of skullcaps
'boys wearing skullcaps'

The construct usually includes two nouns, and so the participle is seen as noun-like. My view is that, as far as FORM is concerned, the participle indeed retains much of its original nature, as I already explained above in detail. By "form" I mean morphology and also co-occurrence specifications. But the reading assigned to that participle is different today. Semantically, the participle in example (3) is perceived as a verb, and the other member of the construct is perceived as a direct object. In support of this reading two syntactic facts are noticed: first, one can add sentence adverbs like *berišul* 'in slovenliness' (carelessly) at the end of the above example. More important, however, is a second fact. Constructs have a homonymous paraphrase with *šel* 'of'. For example, the phrase

(4) *kova hayeled*
the hat of the boy
'the hat of the boy'/'the boy's hat'

can be paraphrased, with the exact meaning retained, as

(5) *hakova šel hayeled*
the hat of the boy
'the hat of the boy'/'the boy's hat'

However, with a participle as the first member of the construct, such a paraphrase is impossible:

(6) *nearim xovšey kipot*
boys wearPAR of skullcaps
'boys wearing skullcaps'

(7) **nearim xovšim šel kipot*
boys wearPAR of skullcaps
'*boys wearing of skullcaps'

Of course, when the participle has been lexicalized as a noun and is perceived as one, such a paraphrase IS possible:

(8) *menael hamifal*
the directPAR of the factory
'the director of the factory'

(9) *hamenael šel hamifal*
the directPAR of the factory
'the director of the factory'

('directPAR' has been lexicalized as a noun).

I conclude that although the form (morphology and valence) of the participle has remained, the MnH participle is a verb and not an intermediate form.

4. Distribution

4.1. Similarity to Infinitives, Gerundives, and 'that' Clauses

Berman also investigates in detail the distribution of the participle. To begin with, she says that the participle can appear in places otherwise reserved for infinitives, gerundives, and 'that' clauses, and that the participle can be paraphrased by such categories. For example:

(10) a.–d. *ani roe oto* { *holex* / *kšeu holex* / *belexto* / *lalexet* }

a.–d. I seePAR him { goPAR / when that he goPAR / in his walk (in his going) / to go }

a.–d. 'I see him { go' / when he goes' / upon his going' / go' }

(10) a.	*ani*	*roe*	*oto*	*holex*
b.				*kšeu holex*
c.				*belexto*
d.				*lalexet*
a.	I	seePAR	him	goPAR
b.				when that he goPAR
c.				in his walk (in his going)
d.				to go
a.	'I see him			go'
b.				when he goes'
c.				upon his going'
d.				go'

Because the proposed paraphrases do so, Berman concludes that the participle receives its time reference from the main verb. That is why it is paraphrased in the 'that' clause, which, being a clause, would include a verb with its own time reference and would not rely on the reference of the higher verb, with a verb whose tense is identical to that of the main verb. The 'that' clause is (10b) above, where the subordinator *še-* 'that' is found in the word glossed 'when that he' (when he).

I propose that the participle in this example should be paraphrased differently than in (10b) and (10c). I do accept (10d) as a paraphrase. Let us examine the 'that' clause, (10b) first. Transformationally speaking, the deep structure of a sentence including a 'that' clause would be

(11) *ani roe [hu holex]*
I seePAR [he goPAR]

from which can be derived the surface structure

(12) *ani roe šeu holex*
I seePAR that he goPAR
'I see that he goes (is going)'

Or, by raising of 'he' to direct object, the following sentence can be derived:

(13) *ani roe oto holex*
I seePAR him goPAR
'I see him go'

This is actually sentence (10a).

However, Berman's paraphrase (10b) is not one of the above two surface structures, (12) and (13). It is in fact a 'when' clause rather than a 'that' clause. A 'when' clause such as this can be present WITH the participle and is not mutually exclusive with it: it is not a paraphrase of it. For example:

(14) *ani roe šeu yašen kšeu yošev bakita*
I seePAR that he sleepPAR when that he sitPAR in the class
'I see that he sleeps when he sits in the class'

By contrast, a 'that' clause cannot be present with the participle:

(15) **ani roe šeu yašen šeu yošev bakita*
I seePAR that he sleepPAR that he sitPAR in the class
'I see that he sleeps that he sits in the class'

Therefore, (12) and not (10b) is the relevant paraphrase.

Now let us see what that new paraphrase, sentence (12), reveals about whether the participle is a full-fledged verb or an "intermediate" form. Notice that in a 'that' clause the tense is not necessarily the same as that of the main verb:

(16)

raiti			*kore*
ani roe	}	*šeu*	{ *kara*
ere			*yikra*
I saw			readPAR
I see	}	that he	{ read (past)
I will see			will read
'I saw			reads'
'I see	}	that he	{ read (past)'
'I will see			will read'

All the combinations in (16) are possible sentences.[9] This is exactly the situation I described in my discussion of the lack of the sequence of tenses rule in Hebrew (section 4.2 above). True, due to historical reasons, there is an idiosyncratic quality to the participle. In transformational terms, only a deep structure with a participle in the embedded sentence (not a deep structure with past or future in that position) can undergo raising of the lower subject to direct object of the main verb. However, this idiosyncrasy does not detract from the verbal quality of the participle. The 'that' sentence, far from proving the non-finiteness of the participle, shows it to be a tensed, finite verb.

Now I examine (10c), the paraphrase with the gerundive. *Belexto* means 'when he goes'; this is not the direct object of 'I see' but rather a time adverbial, which, again, can co-occur with a direct object. For example:

(17)

raiti	*oto*	*boxe*	*belexto*	*habayta*
I saw	him	cryPAR	in his walking	to home

'I saw him cry when he walked home'

Thus, the gerundive in (10c) is not a paraphrase of the participle. The former means 'I see him when he goes', while the latter means 'I see him go'. Also, such usage of gerundive adverbials is rather formal and does not rightly belong in my discussion.

I do accept (10d), the infinitive paraphrase (*lalexet* 'to go'), as a paraphrase of the participle, but not as proof of its non-finiteness. As Berman remarks, most verbs take an infinitive or a 'that' clause as complements, and the infinitive is probably spreading to verbs which used to take the participle. The infinitive can do that because of the historically motivated peculiarity of the participle, namely, its ability to have its deep structure subject raised to object of the main verb. This, and the lack of thessequence of tenses rule in Hebrew, assure that in sentences with participles like 'I seePAR him goPAR' (sentence (13)) the time reference inherent in the participle 'go' is identical with that of the main verb. However, as the sentences in (16) show, the participle does not receive its time reference from the higher verb. The only peculiarity of the participle is that it allows its subject to be raised

[9] Example for the skeptical reader:

maxar	*anase*	*lešaxnea*	*oto*	*likro*	*et*	*hasefer*	*haze.*	*ani*
tomorrow	I will try	to convince	him	to read	ACC	the book	the this.	I

mekave	*šeere*	*lefi*	*tguvato*	*šeu*	*beemet*	*yikra*	*oto*
hope	that I will see	by	his reaction	that he	indeed	will read	it-ACC

'tomorrow I will try to convince him to read this book. I hope that I see by his reaction that he will indeed read it'.

The combination of future main verb with future lower verb is probably the one that arouses the most skepticism in this connection; hence the need for this example.

to direct object, thus producing sentence (10b). In infinitive complements, by contrast (I seePAR him to go', (10d)), the infinitive DOES receive its time reference from the main verb, and so, COINCIDENTALLY, both the infinitive and the participle complements have time references identical with that of the main verb. That, and not a non-finite quality of the participle, is why they are acceptable paraphrases of one another.

Berman also characterizes the action denoted by the participle in the above examples as an action in progress while the action of the main verb happens. Although this characterization is true for participles like 'go', consider the following example:

(18) *šamati* *ota* *yora* *bo*
I heard her shootPAR in him
'I heard her shoot him'

It seems that the progressive quality of the participle depends on the meaning of the verb rather than on the tense assigned to that verb. Once again I find that the participle behaves like a tensed verb.

4.2. Complements of Copula and 'Begin'

Further, with regard to the distribution of the participle, Berman observes that the participle can serve as a complement to "copula type verbs". For example:

(19) a.–d. *dan* {*haya* / *nišar* / *nira* / *nimca*} *omed*

a.–d. Dan {was / remained / was seen / was found} standPAR

a.–d. 'Dan {was / remained / was seen / was found} standing'

Berman finds as a common denominator to all of these verbs the fact that they can take as complements the following categories: NP, AP, locatives, and participles. In this regard, of course, the participle behaves like a nominal. I restrict my discussion to *haya* and *nira*; the others are formal and literary. In my informal usage, *nišar* requires an infinitive complement (*nišar laamod* 'remained to stand' 'remained standing'), and *nimca* takes neither the participle nor the infinitive.

As for *haya* before a participle, I have already presented my analysis of it as an auxiliary rather than a copula (I will soon have further occasion to discuss the difference between the two kinds of *haya*). I therefore do not see *haya* as belonging in the list in (19). As for *nira* 'was seen', it can indeed be followed by a NP, an AP, and a locative, but the reason for this distributional fact is the same as the one for the similarity of distribution between the participle and the infinitive just discussed (in sentences like 'I see him go'). *Nira* 'was seen' is another verb of perception, it is simply the passive form of the verb in (10a), and the same analysis applies to it.

Finally, Berman mentions the fact that the participle can occur as the complement of the verb *hitxil* 'began':

(20) *dan* *hitxil* *oved*
Dan began workPAR
'Dan began working'

where normally an infinitive appears. That, she concludes, points to the non-finite character of the participle. While her reasoning is convincing, I point out that this usage is literary and very unusual in everyday, informal Hebrew. It does show an "intermediate" form quality in the participle, but not in the level of usage with which I am concerned. This concludes the discussion of distribution. We proceed now to other qualities of the participle which Berman regards as pointing to a peculiar status of this form.

5. Circumstantial Adverbials

The "attendant circumstance adverbial" is a construction that Berman describes which is identical to what I have termed the "circumstantial adverbial". An example she cites is

(21)	*hu*	*amad*	*šam*	*bapina,*	*boxe*	*xarišit*
	he	stood	there	in the corner,	cryPAR	silently

'he stood there in the corner, crying silently'

Of course, I am in full agreement with Berman regarding the fact that such usage points to a peculiar quality of the verbal element in it, but once again I say that in informal Hebrew such an adverbial would be very stilted. Rather, one is likely to hear

(22)	*hu*	*amad*	*šam*	*bapina*	*vebaxa*	*bešeket*
	he	stood	there	in the corner	and cried	in silence

'he stood there in the corner and cried silently'

(*xarišit* 'silently' is rather literary also, and I therefore substituted *bešeket* 'in silence' for it.) Once again, then, while Berman's goal is to describe all levels of MnH, including literary or formal usage, mine is different, and so (21) is relevant to her discussion but not to mine. As for the informal (22), of course, it includes no participle at all.

6. Nominal Modifiers

Another use of the participle which points to its non-finiteness, Berman says, is its use as a nominal modifier:

(23)	*kolam*	*šel*	*yeladim*	*šarim*	*baka*	*min*	*hakirot*
	their voice	of	children	singPAR-PL	burst	from	the walls

'the voice of singing children burst through the walls'

She analyzes the participle here as a reduced relative. The argument, then, is that this participle receives its time reference (preceding time, in the example above) from the main verb, 'burst'.

However, consider the following example:

(24)

šloša yeladim { *[šešarim]* → *šarim* / *šešaru* / *šayaširu* } *nixnesu laxeder*

three children { [that singPAR-PL] → singPAR-PL / that sang / that will sing } entered to the room

{ [three children that sing] → 'three singing children / 'three children that had sung / 'three children that would sing } entered the room' (the matter in square brackets in (24a) is the relative before its reduction; the form immediately to its right is the reduced relative.)

Exactly as in the case of the participle after verbs of perception, as in (16), the participle here stands in contrast with past and future, and the time reference assigned to these three forms is concurrent, preceding, and subsequent TO THE MAIN VERB, respectively. I do not propose an analysis of this phenomenon, except to say that, as in the case of verbs of perception, the listener is placed in a frame of time reference where tenses are not pegged on the time of speech but on another point of reference, most likely the main verb. In the above example that point is the action denoted by 'entered', and just as the past and future forms are preceding and subsequent WITH REGARD TO THAT POINT, so the participle is the present tense, or concurrent time, with regard to that very same point in time. Therefore, the participle as a nominal modifier does not receive its time reference from the main verb, but has its inherent reference just as past and future forms have.

7. A Transformational Derivation of the Participle

At the end of her discussion of the data, Berman proposes a transformational derivation for the participle. The deep structure is:

(25) $[_{VP\alpha}\ \underset{[+cop]}{V}\ [_{VP}\ V\ X\ ]\ ]$

This is intended as the deep structure for ALL occurrences of the participle. Where the participle functions as a present tense, and has no accompanying *haya*, such as in *moše holex* 'Moshe goPAR' 'Moshe goes', the $\underset{[+cop]}{V}$, which otherwise gives rise to *haya*, is deleted in the derivation by a rule called the Copula Deletion rule. This very same rule also applies to structures of the form

(26) $[_{VP}\ V\ X\ Y\ ]$

just in case the "V" is marked as [+cop] and has present tense, and the X and Y are complements of that copula. From the deep structure (26) are derived all the "nominal sentences" in Hebrew where no verb nor copula appear in the surface structure. These are sentences of the form *moše meandes* (Moshe engineer) 'Moshe is an engineer'. (The two last examples are mine, A.G.)

It is important to note that Berman regards the *haya* before a verbal participle and the *haya* in a nominal sentence, that is, before a noun or an adjective, as essentially identical. She says, "Copula predicates can typically contain NPs or APs as complements ... they can also typically have VP complements, in which case the V of the complement MUST be in the form of the *benoni*" (Hebrew for what I have been calling the participle, A.G.) (Berman 1978:178).

We can conclude, then, that the structure (25), on which Copula Deletion operates, is a generalized structure of *haya* + participle, quoted above as (26). A deep structure of this nature, of course, marks the participle as essentially different from any verb, since past and future verbs would NOT have a copula in their deep structure. Therefore, although the concern of this study is not the transformational analysis of Hebrew, I must show why I disagree with the analysis that necessitates a copula in the deep structure of every participle.

Before I do that, I must mention that neither Berman nor I see the participle as one lexical category which accepts different roles in the surface structure. I have concluded elsewhere (Gordon 1978) that even two homophonous participles, one used verbally and the other nominally, are listed separately in the lexicon, one as a verb and the other as a nominal. Berman seems to adopt a similar view. She states (Ch. 6) that participles used as agent nouns are not transformationally derived from verbs but are separately listed in the lexicon as nouns. Now, when an active participle is used as a noun it more often than not implies the doer of the action, so Berman would not object to at least the most important part of my view of the lexical representation of the participle. The question that remains, then, is whether the verbal participle is treated in any different way than other verbs in the derivation, i.e. does it always have a *haya* in deep structure. I think not.

My first argument is basically semantic. The participle can be seen as a member of two paradigms (here presented with adverbs to clarify their meaning):

(27) a.	*moše*	*halax*	*lakolnoa*	*etmol*	'Moshe went to the cinema yesterday'
b.	*moše*	*holex*	*lakolnoa*	*axšav*	'Moshe is going to the cinema now'
c.	*moše*	*yelex*	*lakolnoa*	*maxar*	'Moshe will go to the cinema tomorrow'
a.	Moshe	went	to the cinema	yesterday	
b.	Moshe	goPAR	to the cinema	now	
c.	Moshe	will go	to the cinema	tomorrow	

(28) a.	*moše*	*haya holex*	*lakolnoa*	*kol yom*	
b.	*moše*	*holex*	*lakolnoa*	*kol yom*	
c.	*moše*	*yiye holex*	*lakolnoa*	*kol yom*	(Rather literary style)
a.	Moshe	was goPAR	to the cinema	every day	
b.	Moshe	goPAR	to the cinema	every day	
c.	Moshe	will-be goPAR	to the cinema	every day	

a. 'Moshe used to go/would go to the cinema every day'
b. 'Moshe goes to the cinema every day'
c. 'Moshe will (regularly) go to the cinema every day'

The paradigm in (27) includes the simple past, present, and future. The paradigm in (28) includes the iterative or repeated-action meaning. The present tense participles in both paradigms are homophonous, but one can show the difference between the simple and iterative meanings by having different deep structures, with *haya* in the iterative case, and without *haya* in the simple case. This would follow the generalization that the auxiliary adds the repeated action meaning to the verb. However, if *haya* is always present in the deep structure, then the deep structure of the iterative and simple participles would be identical, while nobody would claim an identical deep structure for the iterative and simple PAST, for example.

My second argument is that the *haya* which precedes the participle is different in nature from the *haya* which precedes a noun. Recall that in Berman's deep structure formulas both types of *haya* appear as $\begin{smallmatrix}\text{V}\\ [+\text{cop}]\end{smallmatrix}$, and that one rule deletes both. I will refer to the former type of *haya* as an auxiliary, and to the latter as a copula, with the clear understanding that these are merely labels, and the burden of proof is still on me. To begin with, although the auxiliary never appears in the present (even in iterative cases), the copula may (and in fact sometimes must) appear:

(29)	Copula:	*moše*	*hu*	*more*		
		Moshe	is/he	teacher		
		'Moshe is a teacher'				
(30)	Auxiliary:	*moše*	*(*hu)*	*holex*	*layam*	*kol yom*
		Moshe	(*is/he)	goPAR	to the sea	every day
		'Moshe (*is) goes to the beach every day'				

hu, the third person masculine singular pronoun, has assumed the role of the present tense of the copula (but not the auxiliary) *haya*. Sentence (30), if provided with a comma after the subject, is acceptable in some dialects, but only as a left dislocation, with *hu* as a PRONOUN. By contrast, sentence (29) cannot be seen as a left dislocation. So conclude Berman and Grosu (1976:276-279), and I wholeheartedly agree. Therefore, in the RELEVANT reading, the two sentences exemplify the difference in the use of the two types of *haya*.

The second difference between the auxiliary and the copula is in their behavior in fronting cases, where the copula but not the auxiliary allows the movement. The following example demonstrates this difference. I also give an example with a regular verb. In this example, the copula *haya* behaves like a regular verb more than it does like an auxiliary.

(31) Copula:

hu	*haya*	*more*	⇒
he	was	teacher	

'He was a teacher'

more	*hu*	*haya*	*(aval*	*learcot*	*bivirut*	*lo*	*yaxol)*
teacher	he	was	(but	to lecture	in clarity	not	was able)

'a teacher he was (but he could not lecture clearly)'

(32) Auxiliary:

hu	*haya*	*holex*	⇒
he	was	goPAR	

'he would (used to) go'

**holex*	*hu*	*haya*	*(aval*	*layaad*	*lo*	*higia)*
goPAR	he	was	(but	to the destination	not	arrived)

'go he did (but to the destination he never arrived)'

(33) Regular verb:

hu	*katav*	*mixtav*	⇒
he	wrote	letter	

'he wrote a letter'

mixtav	*hu*	*katav*	*(aval*	*et*	*hainformacia*	*lo*	*gila)*
letter	he	wrote	(but	ACC	the information	not	revealed)

'a letter he wrote (but he never revealed the information)'

The auxiliary and the copula also behave differently in questions, where a participle with an auxiliary requires a "Do Support" of sorts, while a copula or a regular verb do not (the reason being, of course, that the copula, like the regular verb, are main verbs, while the auxiliary is not):

(34) Auxiliary:

ma	*hu*	*haya*	*ose*	*bašana*	*šeavra?*
what	he	was	doPAR	in the year	that passed?

'what did he use to do in the past year?'

As compared to the affirmative:

(35)

hu	*haya*	*holex*	*layam*	*bašana*	*šeavra*
he	was	goPAR	to the sea	in the year	that passed

'he used to go to the beach in the past year'

(36) Copula:

(hašana	*hu*	*xaver*	*kneset,*	*aval)*	*ma*	*hu*	*haya*	*bašana*	*šeavra?*
(the year	he	member of	Knesset,	but)	what	he	was	in the year	that passed?

'(This year he is a member of Parliament, but) what was he in the past year?'

As compared to the affirmative:

(37)

hu	*haya*	*more*	*bašana*	*šeavra*
he	was	teacher	in the year	that passed

'he was a teacher in the past year'

(38) Regular verb: *ma hu katav bašana šeavra?*
what he wrote in the year that passed?
'what did he write in the past year?'

As compared to the affirmative:

(39) *hu katav arbaa maamarim bašana šeavra*
he wrote four articles in the year that passed
'he wrote four articles in the past year'

It is seen that only the auxiliary *haya*, in (34), requires 'doPAR' in the interrogative, which is added just for the question and is not found in the affirmative, whereas the copula *haya* in (36) and the regular verb in (38) do not require such an addition of 'do'. While I am not arguing that copulas are identical to regular verbs, I do say that copulas and auxiliaries are different and must not be grouped in one category despite some simplicity that such grouping might offer the analysis.

My third argument in favor of the position I just expressed has to do with a quasi-paraphrase of *haya*, using the same root in a different verb-pattern. I am referring to the verb *hiva* 'constituted' as in the English *this structure constitutes a dwelling*. The point is that this paraphrastic relationship holds between the COPULA and *hiva*, but not between the AUXILIARY and *hiva*. As copula, *haya* is easily replaced with *hiva* without a significant difference in meaning in the following sentence:

(40) *tirkovet šel šney atomim* {*hi* / *meava*} *pruda šel mayim*
compound of two atoms {is/she / constitutes} molecule of water
'a compound of two atoms {is / constitutes} a molecule of water'

The last example in its 'constitute' version is taken from the dictionary of Even Shoshan (1969:254). Note that like the copula, *hiva* has a present tense form, while the auxiliary *haya* has none. With the auxiliary *haya*, no *hiva* paraphrase is possible:

(41) *moše* {*haya* / **hiva*} *holex layam kol yom*
Moshe {was / *constituted} goPAR to the sea every day
'Moshe {would/used to / *constituted} go to the beach every day'

In conclusion, the deep structure and the derivation of the copula *haya* and the auxiliary *haya* are to be distinguished from one another, and facts true of one do not necessarily show the nature of the other. As for the participle as a simple present tense, it should not have a *haya* attached to it in deep structure, so that it can be distinguished from its iterative or durative counterpart.

This concludes the discussion of the differences between my view and Berman's. Like her, I think that the nominal participle is listed as such in the lexicon and that the verbal participle has idiosyncratic characteristics in terms of its morphology and its valence, but I regard the verbal participle, at least in its spoken Hebrew manifestation, as a finite verb, and not as an "intermediate" form. It is thus possible to see in MnH the end point of the development that this paper traces in the participle through the three main stages of Hebrew.

REFERENCES

Bacher, B. Z.
1969 *Nitzaney hadikduk* [Buds of Grammar]. Trans. by A. Z. Rabinowitz. Jerusalem: Kedem.

Bar-Asher, M.
1972 *Kovetz ma'amarim bilshon hazal* [A Collection of Articles on the Language of our Sages]. Jerusalem: The Hebrew University.

Bendavid, A.
1967 "Biblical Hebrew and Mishnaic Hebrew" [In Hebrew]. Tel Aviv: Dvir.

Bergsträsser, G.
1926 *Dikduk Halashon Haivrit* [A Grammar of the Hebrew Language]. Trans. by M. Ben Asher. Jerusalem: Y. L. Magnes.

Berman, R. A.
1978 *Modern Hebrew Structure.* Tel Aviv: University Publishing Projects.

Berman, R. A. and A. Grosu
1976 "Aspects of the Copula in Modern Hebrew." in Peter Cole (ed.) *Studies in Modern Hebrew Syntax and Semantics*, pp. 265-285. Amsterdam: North Holland Publishing Company.

Blake, F. R.
1951 *A Resurvey of Hebrew Tenses.* Roma: Pontificum Institutum Biblicum.

Chomsky, W.
1967 *Hebrew the Eternal Language.* Jerusalem: Rubin Mass.

Driver, S. R.
1892 *A Treatise on the Use of the Tenses in Hebrew.* London: Clarendon Press.

Encyclopaedia Judaica
1972 "Bible." Vol. 4, pp. 832-836.

Encyclopaedia Judaica
1971 "Hebrew Language." Vol. 16, pp. 1577-1600.

Even-Shoshan, A.
1969 *Hamilon Hehadash* [The New Dictionary]. Jerusalem: Kiryath Sepher.

Gesenius
1855 *Hebrew Grammar.* Ed. by E. Rödinger. Trans. by T. J. Conant. New York: American Book Company.

Givón, T.
1977 "The Drift from VSO to SVO in Biblical Hebrew: the Pragmatics of Tense-Aspect." In Charles Li (ed.), *Mechanism of Syntactic Change,* pp. 181-254. Austin: University of Texas Press.

Gordon, A.
1978 "A Kinetic Model of the Lexicon of Hebrew." Paper presented at the Eighth Annual Conference of the California Linguistics Association, Los Angeles.

Har-Zahab, Z.
1956 *Dikduk Halashon Haivrit* [Hebrew Language Grammar]. Tel Aviv: Mahbarot Lesifrut.

Hughes, J. A.
1970 "Another Look at the Hebrew Tenses." *Journal of Near Eastern Studies* 29:12-24.

Kasovski, C. Y.
1967 *Thesaurus Mishnae* [In Hebrew]. Tel Aviv: Massadah.

Kutscher, E. Y.
1970 "Aramaic." In T. A. Sebeok (ed.), *Current Trends in Linguistics* 6, pp. 347-412. The Hague: Mouton.

Livny, I. J.
1958 *Dikduk Halashon Haivrit Hahadasha Vehayshana* [Grammar of the Old and New Hebrew Language]. Jerusalem: Ahiasaf.

Mandelkern, S.
1971 *Concordantiae Hebraicae Atque Chaldaicae.* Jerusalem: Schocken.

Margolis, M. L.
1948 *The Hebrew Scriptures in the Making.* Philadelphia: Jewish Publication Society of America.

Meek, T. J.
1929 "The Co-ordinate Adverbial Clause in Hebrew." *Journal of the American Oriental Society* 49:157-59.

Mettinger, T. N. D.
1973 "The Hebrew verb system: a survey of recent research." *Annual of the Swedish Theological Institute* 9:65-84.

Murtonen, A. E.
1968 "The prehistoric development of the Hebrew verbal system." *Fourth World Congress of Jewish Studies Papers*, pp. 29-33.

Ogden, G. S.
1971 "Time and the verb *haya* in Old Testament prose." *Vetus Testamentum* 21:451-69.

Peretz, Y.
1967 *The Relative Clause* [In Hebrew]. Tel Aviv: Dvir.

Rabin, C.
1972-74 *Ikarey Toldot Halashon Ha'ivrit* [An Outline of the History of the Hebrew Language]. Jerusalem: The Jewish Agency publications.

--
1960 *Toldot Halashon* [The History of the Language]. Ed. by R. Rozenberg. Jerusalem: Akdamon.

Rubinstein, A.
1952 "A finite verb continued by an infinitive absolute in Biblical Hebrew." *Vetus testamentum* 2:362-67.

Segal, M. H.
1909 *Mišnaic Hebrew and its Relation to Biblical Hebrew and to Aramaic.* Oxford: Horace Hart, Printer to the University.

Steinsaltz, A.
1976 *The Essential Talmud.* London: Weidenfeld and Nicolson.

Weiss, I. H.
1867 *Mishpat Leshon Hamishnah* [The Law of the Language of the Mishnah]. Vienna: Hellmann and Fagelgzang.